My GPS To Success

~Lisa Christiansen

~ᏠᎪᎳᎡ ᏞᎪᏔᎪ

The most significant difference between the Native American world and the world of technological societies is the difference in their relationship to the environment. Much of NLP has arisen from strategies designed to change our "mental maps of reality" and has been designed for application in an environment from which we are largely disconnected. The operational presupposition here is that humans are separate from nature. The environment, whether it's a tropical beach, your past history, your boss, your relationships or the voices in your head, is seen as something to be mastered and manipulated as you climb the ladder toward success, enlightenment, power… or just a better life.

The key principle in the Native American world, on the other hand, is that the environment is spirit. Everything has a spirit. The water has a spirit, the mountain has a spirit, the stars have spirits, the wind, the father sun, the mother moon, all have spirits. And, do you know, they are families just like us! And they all have a participation in our real world. We are all implicated in reality.

So, in search of this 'wisdom' which our technological culture lacks, it becomes obvious that one important place to look is toward cultures that experience 'balance' and 'aesthetics' as qualities arising within an environment which is sacred and in which all things are connected.

As we evolve, and the world around us seems to grow smaller and often more threatening, our need for an understanding of ourselves as global citizens increases. This requires an appreciation for the uniqueness around us. It requires that we be able to see beyond the mask of isolated ego and celebrate the rich cultural diversity the world offers. On our beautiful planet, there are people who talk to stones, who listen to the rain, who learn from the trees, who know the secrets of the waterfalls and the waves…and they are still alive, still with us. Their unique 'species of consciousness' is tremendous resource on our planet

Native American consciousness is a deliberate pattern of thought and behavior designed to focus the mind, integrate the body and spirit, bypass the analytical and security filters of the ego, and accomplish a specific healing or helping purpose. Native American consciousness permits you to live in a world in which everything is alive, everything has a spirit and everything has meaning because Native American's live on purpose from the pre-conscious and sub-conscious governing the conscious mind… and that is an experience that brings richness to your life as a human being. The integration of this world-view into our own lives validates our current reality in a unique way by planting ancient seeds in a modern garden in order to allow a new tree of consciousness to flower there.

Ultimately, our leaders can learn the same lesson that the ancient Inca leaders knew so well…you gain the respect of those you lead by respecting them, then and only then are you truly worthy of their respect.

How should the leader, using the energy of the dialogue, shape the values and success ethics that drive the reputation of the individual? Why is personal energy and strength of character so important when it comes to leadership?

'Personal energy and strength of character ' has within it the potential for healing one's self and, thereby, others. Many people have broken spirits and have suffered from a variety of emotional hurts. Although this is part of being human, enlightened leaders recognize that they also have an opportunity to "help make whole" those with whom they come in contact. In his book, "The Servant as Leader," Robert Greenleaf writes: "There is something subtle communicated to one who is being served and led if implicit in the compact between servant-leader and led is the understanding that the search for wholeness is something they share."

Change is an important factor of life. It can be positive or negative. How can its prefix be influenced by the leader and his leadership energy? Serve, serving is the key to leading.

Preparation Exercises

CONGRATULATIONS ON YOUR DECISION TO STEP UP!

In order to support you in your commitment to take your life to the next level, we have created a few specific exercises designed to enhance your experience.

These are all designed to either refresh or introduce some of the central concepts taught at "My GPS To Success," and are crucial to understanding many of the tools you will learn with My GPS To Success.

Step One: *History of Psychology: Testing What You Know*

In order to take a 'crash course' in the history of psychology, we've given you a MAP of your My GPS To Success. Once you've read the 'History of Psychology,' take the test to see how much you know.

Step Two: *Be An Active Participant In Your Success*

Below is a list of strategically selected engaging lessons to read. We encourage you to complete all the exercises in these chapters as you read through them. Be an active reader engage your mind and your physiology and associate not only to the words on the page, but what meanings they have for you in your life!

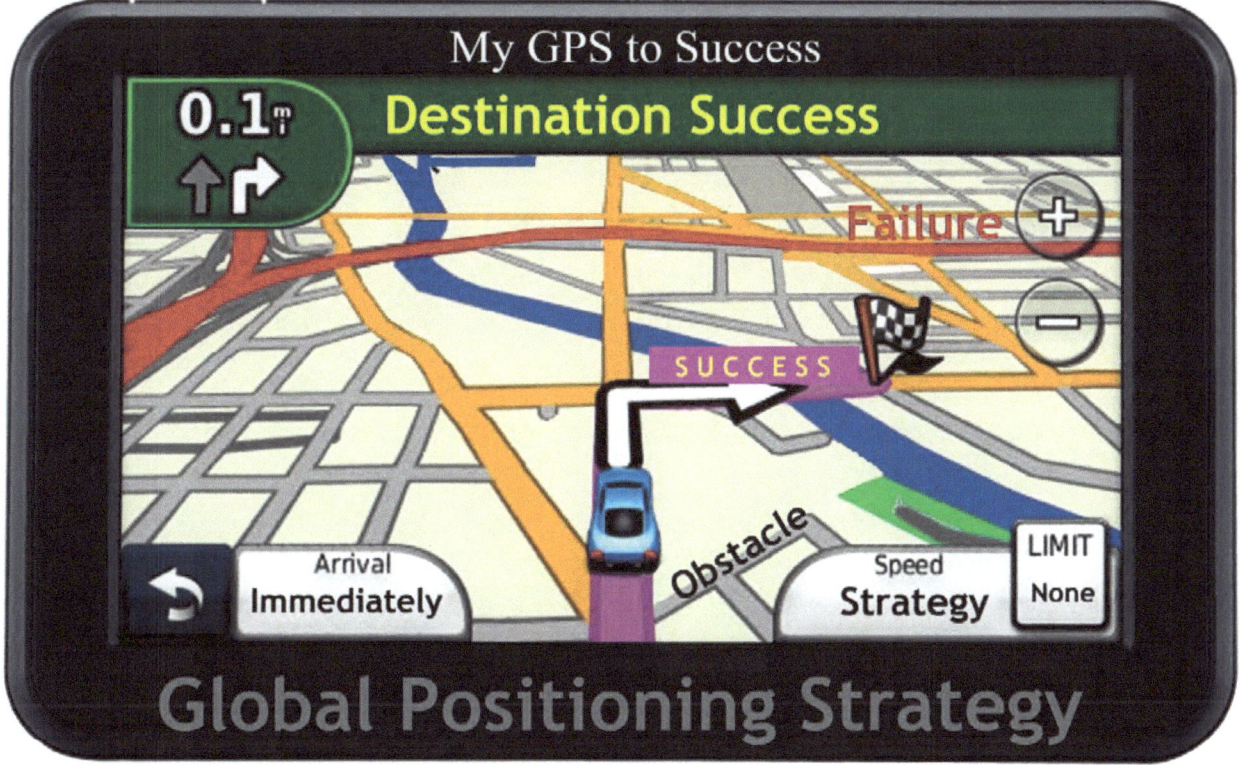

Traditional Psychology:
Models of the Past

The following pages are an overview of five schools of therapy referenced by psychologists and psychiatrists. All of the therapies aim to assist patients with either changing and/or understanding behaviors and emotions. Some of the therapies have a defined time frame for completion or "cure"; others do not. Since the development of psychological theories has clearly been evolutionary, most psychiatrists recognize that no school is the exclusive authority on the human psyche. Therefore, professionals are expected to be capable with many therapeutic techniques, and to be familiar with each of the following schools of thought:

1 Psychodynamic
2 Humanistic
3 Behavioral
4 Cognitive
5 Somatic

```
Definitions:

psychology \sī-kə'-lä-jē\ n

The study of the behavioral and mental processes, including per-
ception and sensation, cognition, learning, and emotions—both the
voluntary and involuntary aspects of human nature.  It focuses on
the study of individuals; although it concerns itself with the
individuals in broader contexts (as parts of a couple, a family,
or a society), the focus is on the processes of the individual.
Its aim is to uncover the "nature of man"—to unravel the mystery
of human hopes, desires, fears, abilities, and limitations.
Psychology is one of many behavioral sciences, borrowing and col-
laborating heavily with other behavioral sciences, such as soci-
ology and anthropology.


psychiatry \sī-kī'-ə-trē\ n

The area of medicine concerned with the diagnosis, treatment, and
study of disordered behavior.
```

Disclaimer: Obviously, not every therapy or nuance of technique can be represented in this document. Categorization of certain therapies is not consistent in the literature so they have been classified as best as possible based on therapy definitions. In addition to examining therapies by school, another approach would be to examine them by patient- or disorder-appropriateness (as in grief counseling, geriatric psychiatry, substance abuse recovery, etc.).

Contemporary Psychiatric Treatment Overview

Regardless of the therapist's particular bias, interviewing the patient is central to clinical psychiatry. The interview may be free-form (determined by the therapist) or standardized (according to a formalized structure).

The following issues are normally covered in the first interview, the diagnostic interview. Subsequent sessions can easily follow the same model of rapport, inquiry, diagnosis, and feedback.

1 Arrange Optimal Conditions
Chairs of the same height and size should be used to maintain equanimity; direct eye contact should be possible; there should be no obstacles between the therapist and patient.

2 Establish Relationship/Rapport
Build trust with the patient by adopting a respectful, compassionate, genuine, and nonjudgmental demeanor. Observe the patient's nonverbal behavior, listen for explicit and implied distress and emotional pain, respond to it with empathy. Follow the patient's lead, and do not redirect the patient for the first five to ten minutes.

3 Obtain Information
The therapist should seek both factual and emotional information. A complete psychiatric history may be taken. In addition, the therapist will ask the following:

- *open-ended questions* that invite narrative answers ("What do *you mean* when you say you are depressed?");
- *closed-ended questions* that invite a yes, no, or short-answer response ("Have you lost weight?", "When was your last drink?");
- *echo questions* that elicit further narrative (Patient: "I'm afraid she'll leave me because of the money." / Therapist: "The money?");
- *double questions* that request two or more responses at once ("Are you sleeping and eating well?");
- *multiple-choice questions* that give the patient a menu of topics ("Do you have nightmares during the week or just on weekends?").

4 Assess Psychopathology
By observing (sometimes testing) and recording the following information, the therapist has the basis for diagnosis and a treatment plan:

- appearance
- judgment
- intelligence
- emotional state
- attention
- memory
- speech
- concentration
- sensorium (interpretation or reception of stimuli, the body of senses)
- psychomotor behavior (muscular action related to mental activity)

5 Provide Feedback
Even if it's too early to give definitive answers, the therapist should acknowledge the obvious question a patient will have at the close of every interview—"You may be wondering what I think about what you've said…" The therapist can define subsequent steps, talk about conclusions or interpretations, or simply express compassion and caring.

Dynamic Psychotherapy

notes...

"No doubt fate would find it easier than I do to relieve you of your illness. But you will be able to convince yourself that much will be gained if we succeed in transforming your hysterical misery into common unhappiness."
— SIGMUND FREUD

#1 — Dynamic Psychotherapy

The Goal:

Dynamic psychotherapy helps patients become aware of the unconscious forces that cause difficulties.

Sigmund Freud's psychoanalysis was the wellspring from which the variety of dynamic disciplines was born. The **dynamic disciplines** emphasize cause-and-effect relationships between motives, drives, and actions—thus the "dynamic" relationship of unconscious and psychological conflict. It was both a behavioral theory and a practice for treating people who exhibited disorders. Although some of the organizing principles of the therapies within this school differ (most either revise or rebel against Freud), the technique of psychoanalysis is generally used by all practitioners of dynamic therapy.

Following are six disciplines of dynamic psychotherapy:

1. Psychoanalysis (Freud)
2. Analytic Psychology (Jung)
3. Individual Psychology (Alder)
4. Holistic Therapy (Horney)
5. Interpersonal Psychology (Sullivan)
6. Transactional Analysis (Berne)

#1 — DYNAMIC PSYCHOTHERAPY

DISCIPLINE 1: PSYCHOANALYSIS

Sigmund Freud (1856-1939) — Born to middle-class, Jewish parents, Freud was the oldest child of his father's second wife. A precocious super-intellectual, he was reading Shakespeare at age eight and was educated in Greek, Latin, French, and German classics. He attended medical school at the University of Vienna, specializing in neurology and psychiatry, and studied with the famous neurologist Jean Charcot in Paris. He also adopted Josef Breuer's "cathartic method" of treatment. Together they published *Studies in Hysteria* (1895), which detailed their **"talking cure"** and was the genesis of psychoanalysis.

The most important significant breakthrough in Freud's personal life, career, and theory was his self-analysis, during which he discovered the importance of the Oedipus Complex (repressed love and hostility toward parents). This period of self-reflection was precipitated by separation from a colleague (who rejected his focus on sexuality in neuroses) and his father's death. During his life and work, many of Freud's students rejected his focus on sexuality and created their own "branches" of psychoanalysis.

Freud was the first person to scientifically explore the unconscious, to systematically study the determinants of behavior in an attempt to understand and cure his patients. He regarded his book, *The Interpretation of Dreams* (1900), as his greatest work.

ORGANIZING PRINCIPLES

- Neurotic symptoms and behavior may be caused by conflicting thoughts, feelings, memories, and impulses. Conflicts may have been caused by childhood experiences. Patients may not be aware of their own conflicts, which can be *unconscious* and, therefore, expressed in an indirect (covert, disguised) form.

- Many unconscious thoughts, feelings, memories, and impulses are related to sexuality; specifically, conflicts created during infancy (the stages of development correspond to sexual development) manifest as neuroses.

- There are three parts of the psyche: the *id* (drives and desires), the *ego* (reason), and the *superego* (self-judgment).

- Most people, no matter how much they suffer, do not want to change. (Freud termed this *resistance*.)

- Dreams often represent latent or repressed wishes. (But, as Freud said, "Sometimes a cigar is just a cigar.")

- Certain changes in a patient are predictable: a freeing from previously misunderstood (or unexplored) internal limitations; more creativity and productivity; greater mastery over internal states and tolerance of anxiety; and a greater capacity to love others without the "baggage" from previous relationships (parental or otherwise).

#1 — Dynamic Psychotherapy

Discipline 1: Psychoanalysis

Therapeutic Technique

NOTE: Only those patients who suffer from symptomatic neuroses of a hysterical, obsessive-compulsive, or phobic nature, or who have anxiety, higher-level personality disorders, and narcissistic personality disorders are considered suitable for psychoanalytic treatment. Those who are pathological liars or criminals are usually not suitable.

- In formal psychoanalysis, patient and therapist meet four or five times a week for 45-50 minutes. Generally, this schedule lasts for a minimum of 100 hours over a number of years.

- Patients lie on a couch with the analyst out of view.

- **Patients engage in** *free association* (which is still the basic tool for exploring the unconscious influences of behavior), telling psychotherapists whatever thought, feeling, or memory enters their minds. Doing so without censorship reveals unconsciously motivated resistance to repressed thoughts and memories, especially sexual ideas.

- Dreams and past experiences are interpreted and examined for universal symbolism and personal meaning.

- Patients are encouraged to experience an unconscious shift of feelings associated with persons in the past to the therapist, i.e., *transference*. This "re-created" relationship can then be used to work out the earlier conflict.

- The analyst interprets and analyzes to help the patient clarify and resolve conflicts.

STRENGTHS	**LIMITATIONS**
_____	_____
_____	_____
_____	_____
_____	_____
_____	_____
_____	_____

#1 — Dynamic Psychotherapy

Discipline 2: Analytic Psychology

Carl Jung (1875-1961) — Throughout his life, Jung experienced dreams and visions filled with remarkable symbolism. These experiences no doubt led to his interest in and development of his theories about archetypes. In addition, **Jung said that he always felt the presence of two distinct personalities within himself: one that acted in the external world and one that acted in the private world where he experienced a closeness to God.** This dual presence formed a basis for much exploration into the idea of an integrated personality.

Jung was educated in Basel, Switzerland, after which he was **closely tied with Sigmund Freud for six years. Nonetheless, Jung broke away from Freud over a dispute about the significance of sexuality in human life.**

His autobiography, *Memories, Dreams, Reflections* (1961), describes in detail **Jung's personal background and reveals the struggles he felt between the differing sides of his personality.**

Organizing Principles

- Archetypal symbols are central to understanding human nature.

- People have **two layers of the unconscious: the personal and the collective.** The *personal unconscious* contains all forgotten or repressed thoughts and feelings, while the *collective unconscious* is an innate structure common to all humans and composed of the archetypes (symbols).

- There is a feminine principle in men—**anima**—and a masculine principle in women—**animus**.

- There is a general creative life energy, the *libido*, which can be invested in a number of different ways. For example, if the libido is invested in the external world, one can be termed an *extrovert*; whereas, if it is invested in the private realm of images, ideas, and so on, one can be termed an *introvert*. The other dichotomies he proposed are *thinking/feeling* and *sensing/intuiting*.

- The deepest layers of the unconscious act independent of time, space, and causality, thus explaining paranormal phenomena.

#1 — Dynamic Psychotherapy

Discipline 2: Analytic Psychology

Therapeutic Technique

NOTE: Jungian techniques are best suited for educated people in dealing with developmental problems of mid-life.

- Jung proposed that therapy should begin with four visits per week, and then be reduced to one to two visits a week. Jungian therapists today meet with patients once a week.

- Patients sit up and face the therapist (as with all therapies described from this point on).

- With the therapist as mediator, a "dialogue" is set up between the conscious mind and the contents of the unconscious mind using free association.

- Patients are made aware of both personal and collective (universal or archetypal) meanings of their symptoms and difficulties.

- In the best of circumstances, a patient begins a process of integrating opposite tendencies to achieve personal "wholesomeness." This process is called *individuation*.

STRENGTHS	LIMITATIONS

#1 — Dynamic Psychotherapy

Discipline 3: Individual Psychology

Alfred Alder (1870-1937)

Organizing Principles

Although he was one of the original members of Freud's circle, Alder rejected Freud's libido theory, that is Freud's insistence on sexual causes for neuroses and infantile wishes. Instead, Alder focused on his own *socially conscious* theory of development.

- **People strive for self-esteem** and to overcome a sense of inferiority; psychological health is equated with positive social consciousness (knowing that the acts of individuals affect larger groups, being aware of the needs of others, the "group mind").

- **People are guided by conscious values and goals, not unconscious instincts.**

- **People move away from situations that make them feel inferior and toward goals that make them feel successful and superior.** An *inferiority complex* is an emotional condition of feeling extremely inferior. (Feelings of inferiority stem from children making unrealistic comparisons between their abilities and those of adults.)

- One's *lifestyle* is the way one sees oneself in the world, one's goals, and one's pathway to those goals. Actual events are not as important as a person's reactions to those events.

- Individuals are a part of larger systems: physical, social, and biological. Problems are resolved in these contexts by developing *social interest* or *social consciousness* (see definition from the first bullet).

- Every failure represents action toward a socially useless goal.

- **Patients are treated in the context of a *whole person* (physical, social, biological), with the focus of building self-esteem and helping them become aware of lifestyle mistakes so that they may be corrected. (In other words, patients are made to feel better about themselves and to reinterpret the world and their place in it.)**

#1 — Dynamic Psychotherapy

Discipline 3: Individual Psychology

Therapeutic Technique

- Frequency of sessions: three per week, tapering off to once a week.

- Patients sit facing the therapist for collaborative, interactive sessions.

- **Individual psychology concerns itself with removing the blocks to living productively in the real world.** Sessions focus first on pointing out mistaken self and world views (lifestyles), then on helping the patient redefine a life goal of social consciousness. This process is done through reeducation and instruction.

- *Reframing* is a technique pioneered by Alder. Patients are made to see things from a different perspective through the observations or ideas offered by the therapist. (For example, instead of viewing indecision as merely weakness and mixed feelings, it is viewed as a desire to maintain the status quo.) After listening to the therapist's alternative viewpoint, the patient is encouraged to take constructive action.

- *Paradoxical communication* is another of Alder's techniques still widely used today. Commonly termed *reverse psychology*, it involves instructing the patient to do the opposite of what the therapist wants him or her to do. (For example, the therapist might suggest to a timid person, "Don't start doing anything too brave.")

STRENGTHS	**LIMITATIONS**
_____	_____
_____	_____
_____	_____
_____	_____
_____	_____
_____	_____
_____	_____

#1 — Dynamic Psychotherapy

Discipline 4: Holistic Therapy

Karen Horney (1885-1952)

Organizing Principles

- In holistic therapy, Freud's psychoanalysis **is reinterpreted to stress security needs over sexual and aggressive drives.** (In this sense, Horney resembles Alder. See *Individual Psychology*.) **Children's needs for security drive them to certain behavior patterns that can lead to inner conflicts and neuroses.**

- **People are always capable of growth and change.**

- Neurotic people have created an idealized image of themselves and expect to be treated as that idealized person instead of who they have presented to the world. They create "shoulds" or irrational, self-imposed demands upon themselves that they rarely if ever fulfill.

Therapeutic Technique

- The therapist talks with the patient in a collaborative, cooperative style.

- Dream analysis is used in all phases of treatment.

- There are three phases of treatment: 1) *disillusioning*, wherein patients come to know what protective blockages (e.g., silence, lateness) have been keeping them from self-realization; 2) *struggle*, wherein patients experience the pain of resolving conflict (e.g., uncertainty, psychic pain, self-hatred); and 3) *discovery*, wherein patients learn how to use their inner self.

STRENGTHS	LIMITATIONS
_____	_____
_____	_____
_____	_____
_____	_____
_____	_____

#1 — DYNAMIC PSYCHOTHERAPY

DISCIPLINE 5: INTERPERSONAL PSYCHOLOGY

Harry Sullivan (1892-1949)

ORGANIZING PRINCIPLES

- Freudian psychoanalysis is paired with perspectives from social psychology, resulting in a de-emphasis on biology and sexuality and, instead, an emphasis on personal relationships.

- Sullivan's personality theory is founded on a premise of two basic human needs: satisfaction and security. The needs for satisfaction include the physical needs (e.g., food, air, water, warmth, etc.) and some emotional needs (e.g., human contact, expressing talent, etc.). Security is the need for lack of anxiety. ***Anxiety*** occurs when there is a fear of needs being unmet.

- Diagnostic labeling is unhelpful, restrictive, and dehumanizing.

THERAPEUTIC TECHNIQUE

- Therapy is divided into four stages: 1) *inception*, which occurs for about 15 minutes of the first session and wherein the therapist and patient define a "contract" (agreement) and their roles; 2) *reconnaissance*, which occurs over as many as 15 sessions and wherein the therapist uncovers the patient's recurring patterns; 3) *detailed inquiry*, wherein the patient and therapist explore the patient's thoughts, feelings, and memories for an unspecified duration; 4) *termination*, which is determined by the patient's assessment of the achievement of goals as defined (and redefined) by the patient and therapist.

STRENGTHS	LIMITATIONS
_____	_____
_____	_____
_____	_____
_____	_____
_____	_____
_____	_____

#1 — DYNAMIC PSYCHOTHERAPY

DISCIPLINE 6: TRANSACTIONAL ANALYSIS

Eric Berne (1910-1970)

ORGANIZING PRINCIPLES

- Transactional analysis is based upon a global metaphor that all people have three "parts", i.e., ***ego states***, within themselves: *parent*—who is authoritarian; *adult*—who is objective; and *child*—who is spontaneous, rebellious, and cooperative.

- The *parent* is the ego state derived from the person's parental figures. In it, the individual acts just as one of his parents did when he was small.

- The *adult* is the objective ego state dealing with the reality of the world.

- The *child* is the ego state of the remainder of the individual responding in its own childlike fashion.

- The primary motivator of people is the need for strokes, which are demonstrations of positive attention from others.

- **The primary purpose of transactional analysis is to gain social control: The individual's *adult* retains primary control of all social situations.**

- **People play** *games* (behavioral patterns with psychological payoffs). For example, "uproar" is a game in which minor incidents lead a couple to fight, resulting in withdrawal. The ulterior motive of this game, which is successfully accomplished, is to avoid sexuality and intimacy between the couple.

- *Scripts* **are the overall way one plays out one's life.** They are usually laid down early in childhood and influenced by culture, family, and parents. **"Script analysis" aids patients in seeing how and why they play a role throughout their lives; then they have the possibility of changing the script.**

- Individuals take four basic life positions: 1) "I'm okay, you're okay"; 2) "I'm okay, you're not okay"; 3) "I'm not okay, you're okay"; 4) "I'm not okay, you're not okay."

THERAPEUTIC TECHNIQUE

- In therapy, patients come to observe and recognize the three basic ego states (parent, child, adult) in themselves and others, and to recognize how these ego states interact with each other. **The therapist must believe in the *adult* of all patients and keep patients aware of their progress**—which stage they have reached and where they are going.

- Because the basic aim of transactional analysis is for self-control in social interactions, group therapy is often useful. However, the therapist can also explore problems in individual sessions if necessary.

#1 — Dynamic Psychotherapy

Discipline 6: Transactional Analysis

Therapeutic Technique (cont.)

- *Regression analysis* **is when the therapist takes on the role of a *child* and interacts with the patient from this position.** Patients experience their own *child*, learning about issues that affect the *child* ego state as well as those of the *adult* and *parent*.

- After the patient has attained maximum benefit from structural analysis: 1) therapy can be terminated permanently or for a trial period; **2) therapy can be followed with psychoanalysis**; or 3) the patient can be placed in transactional analysis, usually within the context of a group.

- Following transactional analysis, proper game analysis (useful for attaining social control) and script analysis (designed for long-term control) can be employed, along with a continued use of transactional analysis.

- After patients are made aware of their selves, the therapist and patient will often set up a bilateral contract focusing on changes the patient wishes to make, outlining possible changes and methods of change. It is up to the patient, not the therapist, to decide what is to be changed; work will continue with the therapist and group to gain intellectual and emotional insights.

- Technical points: 1) The therapist should always have examples from the patient's experience to explain a diagnostic point; **2) If historical material cannot be found, the diagnosis should be held off**; 3) Terms such as *childlike* and *immature* should not be used to describe actions; 4) For best results in therapy, it is necessary for the patient to experience the ego state of the child, not just understand it intellectually.

STRENGTHS

_____

_____

_____

_____

_____

_____

LIMITATIONS

_____

_____

_____

_____

_____

_____

notes...

"We are much more simply human than otherwise."
HARRY SULLIVAN, COMMENTING ON SCHIZOPHRENIA

Humanistic Therapy

notes...

#2 — Humanistic Therapy

The Goal:
Humanistic therapy assists the patient in moving toward self-improvement.

Humanistic therapies (focusing on the humanness of people and their tendency toward self-actualization) represent a general approach to **understanding human beings**, and are not based on preconceived ideas about the present condition or past life of the patient. They are based on an **optimistic view of people and the assumption that patients can improve through their own effort with some guidance from the therapist.** The therapist gives aid and some direction, but the patient holds the key to success in the therapy. Therapists' activities vary among the different therapies. Emphasis is placed on the patient's feelings; the therapist works to redirect these feelings.

Humanistic therapists must follow the tenets set forth by the **Humanistic Creed**: 1) Have a fundamental respect for patients and see them as active agents capable of change; and 2) Perceive each patient as an individual with whom one must have an interpersonal relationship for the therapy to be effective.

Following is an overview of the three humanistic therapies:

1. Client-Centered/Nondirective Psychotherapy (Rogers)

2. Existential (Binswanger, Frankl, Maslow, et al.)

3. Gestalt (Perls, Lewin, et al.)

#2 — HUMANISTIC THERAPY

DISCIPLINE 1: CLIENT-CENTERED THERAPY/NONDIRECTIVE PSYCHOTHERAPY

Carl Ransom Rogers (1902-1987) — Born in Oak Park, Illinois, Rogers was a leader in the scientific study of psychotherapy. He was educated at the University of Wisconsin, Union Theological Seminary, and Teachers College at Columbia University.

Early in his career, **Rogers worked as a psychologist for and director of the Child Study Department of the Society for the Prevention of Cruelty to Children.** After 12 years there, he returned to university life and eventually became director of the counseling center at the University of Chicago, where **he studied the effectiveness of his client-centered therapy with schizophrenic patients.** However, **his theories were constructed within the context of work with students, people with relatively minor maladjustments.**

Rogers was a prolific writer, publishing five books on psychology, among them, *On Becoming a Person* (1961) and *Freedom to Learn for the Eighties* (1983).

NOTE: Although Rogers' therapeutic technique was tested with schizophrenics, its application to people who have more than minor maladjustments is still debatable.

ORGANIZING PRINCIPLES

- **The objectives are to help patients (whom Rogers called *clients*) trust and find new meaning** in experience, base decisions on new evidence (references provided either by the therapist or by the clients themselves), and have a more fulfilling life.

- The therapy environment determines clients' ability to achieve these objectives, so the therapist must create a relationship conducive to their growth. Specifically, the therapist must 1) be genuine (sincere, without a facade); 2) accept the experiences of both him-/herself and the client; and, 3) be understanding.

- Everyone experiences life differently. This personalized interpretation is more important than objective reality.

- Unlike Freud, who believed that the impulses of the id were ultimately destructive, Rogers (and the rest of the humanists) believed that humans are basically good.

- The treatment period, although unspecified, is considered "brief," as opposed to the years-long treatment of psychoanalysis or other dynamic psychotherapies.

- The therapist provides a supportive, nonjudgmental understanding but does not advise, interpret for, or direct the client.

#2 — Humanistic Therapy

Discipline 1: Client-Centered Therapy/Nondirective Psychotherapy

STRENGTHS

_____
_____
_____
_____
_____
_____
_____
_____
_____

LIMITATIONS

_____
_____
_____
_____
_____
_____
_____
_____
_____

#2 — Humanistic Therapy

Discipline 2: Existential Therapy

Abraham Maslow (1908-1970) — One of the few in his profession to study healthy individuals, particularly those whom he called "self-actualizers" (high achievers and others who enjoyed "peak experiences" such as creativity, awe, even contemplation), Maslow created a unique theory of human motivation and rejected the dominant American schools of behaviorism and psychoanalysis. This was the birth of *humanism*.

Maslow classified man's basic needs into the categories of abundancy and deficiency. The abundancy needs are those found in the self-actualizers, and are comprised of self-realization, knowing, and understanding, as well as aesthetics. The deficiency needs arise out of insecurity and alienation.

Further, he divided human needs into the following classifications: *physiological* (food, water, sex, sleep), *safety* (protection, security), *love and belongingness, self-respect, self-esteem from others, and aesthetics* (beauty, truth, justice, self-actualization). Humans, he proposed, live at the lowest level of problem. In other words, if food and water are a concern, the person will live in the realm of physiological needs; however, if these needs have been provided, then the person will live in the realm of safety, and so on.

This first "humanist" was born in Brooklyn, New York, and educated at the University of Wisconsin. His major publications include *Motivation and Personality* (1954), *Toward a Psychology of Being* (1962), and *Religion, Values and Peak Experiences* (1964).

NOTE: Some notable contemporaries of Mr. Maslow's include Ludwig Binswanger (1881-1966), Victor Frankl (1905-1997), and Rollo May (1909-1994).

Maslow's Hierarchy of Needs

Maslow arranges motives in a hierarchy ascending from such basic physiological needs as hunger and thirst to safety to love to self-esteem (e.g., feeling competent), and ultimately, to self-actualization—the full realization of one's human potential, as in creativity. The lower needs are more powerful and demand satisfaction first. The higher needs have less influence on behavior, but are more distinctly human. Generally, higher needs do not become a focus until lower ones have been at least partly satisfied.

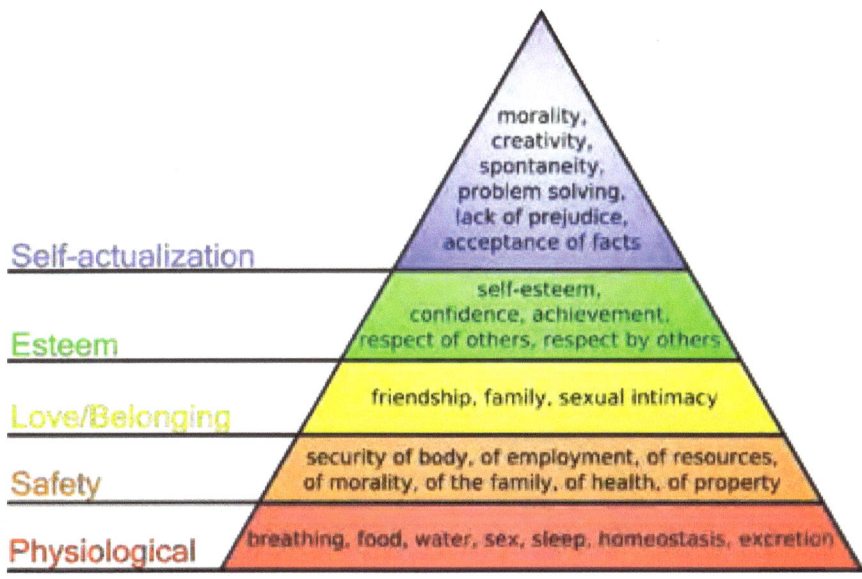

#2 — Humanistic Therapy

Discipline 2: Existential Therapy

Organizing Principles

- **Based on the existential philosophy that humans are *emerging* and *becoming*, rather than being a collection of mechanisms or dynamics, existential therapy is an attempt to meld the patient's perception of reality with objective reality.**

- Overall, it is impossible to delineate specific existential techniques of therapy; **it is more an orientation or attitude toward others that therapists adopt** and use to guide their work with patients.

- The aim of therapy is not to alleviate a symptom or help the patient "adjust" to society, but rather to have the patient discover his or her own being (self-experience). When the therapy is successful, **patients *must* experience their existence as real**; they become fully aware of this existence so that options and potentials become evident and change is seen as possible.

- Frankl's *logotherapy* emphasizes that humans' most fundamental motive is to find meaning in life.

- Binswanger delineated three different modes of the world for each person, which aided therapists in understanding the individual: the *Umwelt*, or nonpersonal biological environment; the *Mitwelt*, or world of fellow beings and social relationships; and the *Eigenwelt*, the private world of self-identity. Binswanger applied this concept to the full continuum of human behavior from normal to neurotic to psychotic.

- **The patient's life history is seen as his or her way of being in the world.** Each person is a completely unique individual with a unique background that plays an important role in his or her present being.

> "A musician must make music, an artist must paint, a poet must write, if he is to be ultimately at peace with himself. What a man can be, he must be."
> — Abraham Maslow, from *Motivation and Personality* (1954)

#2 — HUMANISTIC THERAPY

DISCIPLINE 2: EXISTENTIAL THERAPY

THERAPEUTIC TECHNIQUE

- Therapists must be flexible in their use of techniques, which are primarily the same as those of psychodynamic therapists (see *Freud*). In other words, free-association or other techniques may be used—indeed, *any* technique that meets the objectives may be used.

- Therapy is understood as an encounter between two individuals who optimally treat each other as subjects, not objects.

- Both individuals must feel that they are participating in and that most of the work of therapy is being accomplished in the encounter. **The therapist does not direct the patient, but is an existential partner to the patient, helping reestablish communication with self and others that have been lost in some way.**

- **Dreams are not interpreted**; they are seen as one manifestation of the individual's being in the world.

- **No assumptions are made about the meaning of past incidents.** The meaning can only be discovered by working with the patient.

STRENGTHS	LIMITATIONS
_____	_____
_____	_____
_____	_____
_____	_____
_____	_____
_____	_____
_____	_____
_____	_____

#2 — HUMANISTIC THERAPY

DISCIPLINE 3: GESTALT THERAPY

Frederick "Fritz" Perls (1922-1990); Kurt Lewin (1890-1947); et al.

ORGANIZING PRINCIPLES

- Neuroses come from repressing a "part of the whole" (*gestalt* is German for *whole*). By reliving painful experiences, neuroses can be healed.

- Gestalt theory is organized around the following three perspectives:
  1. **Phenomenological:** events in the here and now; e.g., whatever exists and is experienced here and now is more reliable than interpretation of the past.
  2. **Field Theory:** motivation and social factors; e.g., needs increase in volume until they are satisfied, and well-adjusted people experience a constant flow of need and satisfaction.
  3. **Existential:** "being" in the here and now.

- The goal of the phenomenological perspective is insight, which is achieved through focused awareness and experimentation; with insight, an accurate perception of oneself, one's needs, and the world is possible.

- The field theory perspective emphasizes the holistic relationship of the field (the person and his or her "life space") to the environment. Events become meaningful only when one knows the frame of reference of the observer.

- The existential perspective is based on phenomenology. **The goal is to be "authentic" and responsible for oneself. People are remaking or discovering themselves endlessly.**

#2 — HUMANISTIC THERAPY

DISCIPLINE 3: GESTALT THERAPY

THERAPEUTIC TECHNIQUE

- **The focus is on awareness of what is and encourages thinking that supports experience.**

- The therapist and patient engage in an "existential dialogue": a warm, caring conversation based on experiencing one another as they really are.

- The characteristics of this dialogue are 1) **inclusion**—empathy without judgment, analysis, or interpretation, while retaining self-awareness; 2) **presence**—the therapist and client both express thoughts and feelings throughout the dialogue; 3) **commitment to dialogue**—*the therapist commits to this interpersonal process rather than a therapeutic outcome;* and 4) **living dialogue**—all modalities are explored to enhance the dialogue, such as dancing, songs, and words.

- Role-playing is used. Patients may imagine that a person with whom they have a conflict is sitting in an empty chair. The patient then talks to the chair and imagines the responses.

STRENGTHS	LIMITATIONS
_____	_____
_____	_____
_____	_____
_____	_____
_____	_____
_____	_____
_____	_____
_____	_____

Behavioral Therapy

notes...

#3 — Behavioral Therapy

The Goal:

Behavioral therapy emphasizes changing specific maladaptive behaviors in precise and measurable ways.

Behavior therapies were originally developed from "accidental" discoveries made by Ivan Pavlov and others (John B. Watson, 1879-1958; B.F. Skinner, 1904-1990; Joseph Wolpe, 1915-1997; et al.) in experimental psychology and physiology labs.

Early proponents believed behavior was totally determined by environmental stimuli. Current behavior therapists, however, recognize the importance of cognition, feelings, and social interaction in the control of human behavior, and stress the importance of self-control and self-direction in altering behavior. They increasingly rely on all relevant aspects of experimental psychology, not only on learning psychology.

#3 — Behavioral Therapy

John B. Watson (1879-1958) — "Father" of the behaviorist movement, he coined the term *behaviorism.* While performing certain animal experiments as a doctoral student at the University of Chicago, Watson noted that some data (e.g., overt acts) could be verified reliably by other psychologists, whereas other data (e.g., the supposed mental state of the animal) could not be so verified. **Watson theorized that introspection was a faulty method and urged that scientific psychological research be limited to observing overt acts.**

Burrhus F. Skinner (1904-1990) — Skinner was primarily interested in instrumental conditioning, which he termed *operant conditioning.* **Skinner was not concerned with *why* a particular stimulus is reinforcing or punishing; he was interested only in *how* environmental consequences shape behavior.** Skinner and his students clarified the concepts of *contingencies of reinforcement* and *schedules of reinforcement*, noting that different schedules strengthen or weaken learning differentially.

John Wolpe (1915-1997) — After he studied learning processes, Wolpe devised new techniques based on observable behavior, including *systematic desensitization.* In 1958, he published *Psychotherapy by Reciprocal Inhibition*, considered to be the most influential work espousing behavioral techniques (although he did not use the term *behavior therapy*) that had yet appeared. In 1969, **Wolpe claimed that there are three reasons for failure in behavior therapy: 1) faulty analysis of the case; 2) improper choice or application of technique; and 3) lack of proper technique for the case in the therapist's tool kit.**

> "We are all controlled by the world in which we live, and part of that world has been and will be constructed by men. The question is this: Are we to be controlled by accidents, by tyrants, or by ourselves...?"
> — B.F. Skinner, from *Cumulative Record* (1959)

#3 — BEHAVIORAL THERAPY

ORGANIZING PRINCIPLES

- **Behavior disorders are learned behaviors that are maladaptive** in the life of the individual; *they are not caused by unconscious conflict,* lack of insight, lack of positive regard, or any other such concept. *The symptom is itself the disorder.*

- Natural behavior responses can be conditioned to appear upon the occurrence of another stimulus not usually associated with the appearance of the response. The first element necessary, however, is a previously established reflex that consists of a stimulus and response, whereby the stimulus reliably elicits the response.

  (*Classical conditioning* was discovered by Ivan Pavlov [1849-1936], who had originally set out to study the physiology of the secretion of digestive fluids in the mouth and stomach of dogs, but noted that, after a period of time, the dogs would secrete juices as soon as he walked into the room.)

- *Instrumental conditioning* is described as a connection that is established between a behavior and the reinforcement or punishment that *follows* it. **Behavior is thus viewed as a function of the consequences of the behavior, and behavior change is a function of a change in the consequences.**

  E.L. Thorndike (1874-1949) discovered the "law of effect", which states that if a behavior is followed by rewarding consequences, it becomes more probable that under similar circumstances, the behavior will occur again.

  In 1970, **Howard Rachlin concluded that there are four basic principles of instrumental conditioning:**

  1. Reward;
  2. Punishment (the response is followed by painful or aversive stimuli);
  3. Escape or negative reinforcement (the response is followed by the removal of an aversive stimulus);
  4. **Omission (the reward is absent after the response).**

- *Observational or social learning theory:* American psychologists, especially Albert Bandura, Walter Mischel, and Julian Rotter, are developing a new paradigm that considers the common sense observation that people learn not only by doing, but also by observing the behavior of models, either in the real world or through various media.

  Observational learning is affected by numerous variables, including 1) the similarity of the model to the subject; 2) the type of behavior exemplified by the model; 3) the consequences of the model's behavior; and, 4) the motivation given to the subject.

#3 — BEHAVIORAL THERAPY

THERAPEUTIC TECHNIQUE

- Behavioral therapists assume more control over the treatment sessions and the outside life of the client than do other types of therapists (i.e., humanistic and dynamic). They consider themselves experts and take responsibility for the outcome of the treatment.

- **Behavior therapy of all types basically proceeds in the following four steps:**
  1. Analysis of the maladaptive behavior: Patients can rarely articulate a highly specific, focused problem. Therapists must be able to help, through skillful assessment and careful history-taking, clients pinpoint which behaviors need changing and which variables seem to be causing the behaviors.
  2. Choice of technique: Unlike most other types of therapists, behavior therapists have a wide range of techniques from which to choose. Choice of technique is based on the nature of the problem itself. Therapists usually select a group of techniques that will probably be effective, and try them in turn until success is achieved.
  3. Preparation of the client for treatment: The therapist explains the rationale or ground rules of a technique, gives preparatory "homework assignments", and ensures that the client's expectations are realistic.
  4. Application of the treatment technique chosen, ongoing evaluation, and changes in technique as needed.

- Techniques may include, but are not limited to *counterconditioning through systematic desensitization, behavioral rehearsal, assertive training, operant conditioning, modeling, token economy, covert* (thought process) *control, and aversive behavior techniques* (e.g., electric shock, drugs, etc.).

  The following techniques are those most widely used.
  1. **Token Economy:** Positive reinforcement (rewards or tokens) is used whenever a person performs desired behaviors.
  2. **Aversion Therapy:** An unpleasant stimulus (e.g., shock, odor) is paired (or imagined to be paired) with the undesired behavior.
  3. **Systematic Desensitization:** The patient constructs a "hierarchy" of unpleasant situations (e.g., for a person afraid of flying: going to the airport, getting on the plane, hearing the announcements, taking off, etc.). Then, the patient imagines each situation, progressing from least to most fearful as anxiety diminishes.
  4. **Flooding:** The patient is exposed to (or imagines) the anxiety-producing stimulus. For example, someone afraid of heights would go directly to the top of a tall building.

#3 — Behavioral Therapy

Therapeutic Technique

STRENGTHS   **LIMITATIONS**

notes...

Cognitive Therapy

#4 — Cognitive Therapy

The Goal:

Cognitive psychology explores the higher mental processes including attention, creativity, memory, perception, problem-solving, thinking, and use of language.

While behaviorism sees us as mechanistic beings and humanism sees us as emotional beings striving toward self-actualization, **cognitive therapists see us as a *thinking* system**. Thoughts are what lead to maladaptive behavior. It has been most successfully applied to those with moderate, non-psychotic depression. Much as we view the functions of a computer, the human mind is considered a structured system for handling information: the senses receive stimuli and the mind analyzes, stores, recodes, decodes, encodes, and then uses that information.

Following are two forms of cognitive therapy:

1. Rational-Emotive Therapy (Ellis)
2. Psycholinguistics (Chomsky, et al.)

#4 — Cognitive Therapy

Discipline 1: Rational-Emotive Therapy

Albert Ellis (1913-present)

Organizing Principles

- Patients gain *rational self-acceptance* when they become empowered to manage emotional problems effectively.

- The past cannot be changed, but its influence need not sabotage our present and future life.

- Emotions are involved in almost every aspect of our lives, so the *quality* of our emotions is the focus; we can minimize the irrational, debilitating feelings that interfere with thinking and action.

- **As core irrational beliefs begin to change, patients learn new ways of feeling and behaving and begin to experience taking charge of their own lives.**

Therapeutic Technique

- Present attitudes, painful emotions, and maladaptive behaviors are the focus, and a practical, action-oriented solution is the objective. Patients are helped to accept themselves unconditionally and to operate from responsible self-interest rather than selfishness.

- As a patient's self-acceptance increases, **the therapist encourages acceptance of hardships and imperfections, building a high frustration tolerance,** and developing perseverance, patience, and resilience.

- The therapist must establish a supportive, facilitative relationship with clients and collaborate with them to identify problems. **As such, the therapist may design a number of emotional and behavioral methods for helping patients recognize and modify irrational or useless aspects of their beliefs.**

    The strategies may include 1) imagery; 2) "homework assignments" on assertiveness, self-nurturing, risk-taking, etc.; 3) communication skills; and, 4) "shame attacking" exercises.

STRENGTHS   LIMITATIONS

_____   _____

_____   _____

_____   _____

_____   _____

#4 — Cognitive Therapy

Discipline 2: Psycholinguistics

Noam Chomsky (1928-present)

Organizing Principles

- Psycholinguistics grew out of the psychologists' interest in linguistics, and the linguists' interest in psychology.
- *Phonetics* is the study of the phonemes ("sounds") of a language: how words come together and what affect they have on us.
- *Syntax* is concerned with the sequence of words and what affect it can have on us.
- *Semantics* is concerned with the role of meaning and the analysis of morphemes (the smallest units of speech that have meaning).
- According to B.F. Skinner (see *Behavioral Therapy*), language behavior is the same as any other learned behavior: It can be conditioned with rewards and reinforcement.
- There is a distinction between *performance* (actual processes) and *competence* (knowledge and ability) and between *deep* (meaningful) and *surface* (presented) structures of language.

Therapeutic Technique

- Therapies based on psycholinguistics are widely varied and are practiced by psychologists, psychiatrists, and nonmedical professionals. Pioneers in the field of linguistics as therapy include Virginia Satir, Richard Bandler, and John Grinder (see next page).

STRENGTHS	LIMITATIONS
_____	_____
_____	_____
_____	_____
_____	_____
_____	_____
_____	_____

#4 — Cognitive Therapy

REFERENCE

Neuro-Linguistic Programming (NLP)

According to Robert B. Dilts, NLP is a behavioral model and a set of explicit skills and techniques founded by John Grinder and Richard Bandler in 1975. Defined as *the study of the structure of subjective experience*, NLP studies the patterns or *programming* created by the interaction between the brain ("neuro"), language ("linguistic"), and the body, which produces both effective interactive procedures and ineffective behavior in order to better understand the processes behind human excellence. The skills and techniques were derived by observing the patterns of excellence in experts from diverse fields of professional communication including psychotherapy, business, hypnosis, law, and education.

Historical Overview of NLP

The name NLP encompasses the three most influential components involved in producing experience: neurology, language, and programming. The neurological system regulates how our bodies function; language determines how we interface and communicate with other people; and our programming determines the kinds of models of the world we create. NLP describes the fundamental dynamics between mind (neuro) and language (linguistics), and how their interplay effects our body and behavior (programming).

NLP was originated by John Grinder (whose background was in linguistics) and Richard Bandler (whose background was in mathematics and Gestalt therapy) for the purpose of making explicit models of human excellence. Their first work, *The Structure of Magic Vol. I* and *II* (1975, 1976), identified the verbal and behavioral patterns of therapists Fritz Perls (the creator of Gestalt therapy) and Virginia Satir (internationally renowned family therapist). Their next work, *Patterns of the Hypnotic Techniques of Milton H. Erikson, M.D. Vol. I* and *II* (1975, 1976), examined the verbal and behavioral patterns of Milton Erikson, founder of the American Society of Clinical Hypnosis and one of the most widely acknowledged and clinically successful psychiatrists of our time. As a result of this earlier work, Grinder and Bandler formalized their modeling techniques and their own individual contributions under the name "Neuro-Linguistic Programming" to symbolize the relationship between the brain, language, and the body. The basics of this model have been described in a series of books including *Frogs into Princes* (Bandler and Grinder, 1979), *Neuro-Linguistic Programming Vol. I* (Dilts, Grinder, Bandler, DeLozier, 1980), *Reframing* (Bandler and Grinder, 1982), *Using Your Brain* (Bandler, 1985), and *Introducing Neuro-Linguistic Programming* (O'Connor and Seymour, 1990).

Principles of NLP

NLP is a pragmatic school of thought—an "epistemology"—that addresses the many levels involved in being human. NLP is a multidimensional process that involves strategic thinking and an understanding of the mental and cognitive processes behind behavior. NLP provides tools and skills for the development of states of what human beings are, what communication is, and what the process of change is all about. At another level, NLP is about self-discovery, exploring identity, and mission. It also provides a framework for understanding and relating to the "spiritual" part of human experience that reaches beyond us as individuals to our family,

#4 — Cognitive Therapy

REFERENCE

Neuro-Linguistic Programming (NLP)

Principles of NLP (cont.)

community, and global systems. NLP is not only about competence and excellence, it is about wisdom and vision.

In essence, all of NLP is founded on two fundamental premises.

1. **The Map Is Not the Territory.**
   As human beings, we can never know reality. We can know only our perceptions of reality. We experience and respond to the world around us primarily through our sensory representational systems. It is our "neuro-linguistic" maps of reality that determine how we behave and that give those behaviors meaning, not reality itself. It is generally *not* reality that limits us or empowers us, but rather our map of reality.

2.. **Life and "Mind" Are Systematic Processes.**
   The processes that take place within a human being and between human beings and their environment are systematic. Our bodies, our societies, and our universe form an ecology of complex systems and sub-systems all of which interact with and mutually influence each other. It is not possible to completely isolate any part of the system from the rest of the system. Such systems are based on certain "self-organizing" principles, and naturally seek optimal states of balance or homeostasis.

All of the models and techniques of NLP are based on the combination of these two principles. In the belief system of NLP, it is not possible for human beings to know objective reality. Wisdom, ethics, and ecology do not derive from having the one "right" or "correct" map of the world, because human beings are not capable of making one. Rather, the goal is to create the richest map possible that respects the systematic nature and ecology of ourselves and the world in which we live. The people who are most effective are the ones who have a map of the world that allows them to perceive the greatest number of available choices and perspectives. NLP is a way of enriching the choices you have and those you perceive as available in the world around you. Excellence comes from having many choices. Wisdom comes from having multiple perspectives.

According to NLP, the basic process of change involves 1) finding out what the present state of the person is; 2) adding the appropriate resources (to lead that person to...); 3) the desired state.

Present State + Appropriate Resources = Desired State

#4 — Cognitive Therapy

REFERENCE

Neuro-Linguistic Programming (NLP)

Principles of NLP (cont.)

The distinctions and techniques of NLP are organized to help identify and define present states and desired states of various types and levels, and then to access and apply the appropriate resources to produce effective and ecological change in the direction of the desired state.

Through the years, NLP has developed powerful tools and skills for communication and change in a wide range of professional areas including counseling, psychotherapy, education, health, creativity, law, management, sales, leadership, and parenting.

NLP Techniques

The function of any NLP technique is to enrich or add to one of the three properties of effective behavior which are to have 1) an explicit representation of the outcome; 2) a sensory experience; or, 3) flexibility of internal responses and external behavior.

The many explicit techniques and procedures that make up the behavioral technology of NLP are presented in the ever-growing number of books that represent the development of the field of NLP. There are also many techniques that have not been transformed into written representations, and many still in the process of being refined and developed.

1. Identify and match the most commonly used sensory-based words and predicates of another person for the purposes of creating rapport and ensuring understanding.

2. Pace through matching and mirroring of postural, gestural, and facial positions and movements, and of voice tone and tempo qualities of another person, in order to attain rapport with that person.

3. Translate experiences expressed through one representational modality to another in order to help increase understanding between individuals or groups having difficulty communicating with one another.

4. Observe and utilize sensory accessing and minimal cues to help understand and pace another person's typical processing strategies for organizing and making sense of his or her experiences and communications received from others.

5. Help to build new representational possibilities and capabilities in others through the use of sensory specific language and systematic use of accessing cues.

6. Help to increase sensory awareness in order to more accurately and immediately perceive and evaluate the effects of people's behaviors on one another.

#4 — Cognitive Therapy

Reference

Neuro-Linguistic Programming (NLP)

NLP Techniques (cont.)

7. Identify and sort out multiple (incongruent) communications in others in order to help reduce misunderstanding and confusion.

8. Establish anchors and triggers for positive experiences and resources that occur in one context, and retrigger or resequence them to other situations where they are not yet available to a particular individual or group. As a result, those behaviors and responses may serve as resources in other contexts as well.

9. Identify and break unuseful "calibrated loops" between individuals and groups in order to add more flexibility and choice in responses and communication.

10. Break down unspecified verbal maps into higher quality verbal descriptions and, more importantly, behavioral demonstrations and examples, in order to create easily shared and observable representations of a person's experiences and outcomes.

11. Frame and reframe problematic behaviors and responses by making the positive intentions and positive by-products underlying them more explicit. The purpose of this technique is to create a shift in the perceptions of people, with respect to the behavior, so that the behavior may be handled more resourcefully. The shift in perception functions to...

    a. Separate "self" from "behavior" through the reinforcement and validation of the individual as a person by associating the "self" with the positive intent. Any negative responses may then be directed toward the behavioral manifestation rather than the person him-/herself.

    b. Preserve the positive intent of the problematic behavior even though the behavioral means to secure the positive intention are altered.

    c. Preserve and validate the positive by-product of the behavior or response, which serves to help preserve the ecology of the system, as well as validating the "self" while changing the unwanted behavior.

12. Create and reinforce flexibility in the members of a system through role-playing and other forms of behavior modeling to help the members of the system more consistently and systematically elicit desired behaviors and responses from other members.

13. Elicit and detail a high-quality description and demonstration of a group or individual's desired state(s) that will be well-formed, practical, and ecological for the particular system to which they belong.

notes...

Somatic Therapy

notes...

#5 — SOMATIC THERAPY

THE GOAL:

Somatic (from *soma*, Greek for "body") therapies address disorders by treating the physical body.

In many mental disorders it is helpful to think of a continuum from purely psychological causes and symptoms (e.g., death of a loved one, feelings of low self-esteem) to purely biological causes and symptoms (e.g., neurochemical imbalance, sleep disturbance) with all combinations in between.

Somatic therapy holds that, just as most purely psychological problems are not helped by medication, most biologically based psychiatric disorders require medical intervention. **A wide variety of behavioral disorders, ranging from shyness (i.e., social phobia) and learning disabilities (e.g., attention deficit disorder) to clearly biochemical disturbances (e.g., bipolar disorder, schizophrenia) have been considered to have biological components warranting medical treatment.**

Mental patients in the 1700s were considered to have incurable diseases. They were confined to public asylums where they were subjected to harsh measures, such as physical restraint and abuse. More humane treatment was pioneered toward the end of the century by several physicians in Italy, England, and France.

Following are three forms of somatic therapy:

1. *Drug treatment* or the use of psychotropic drugs (those affecting the mind, emotions, and behavior) are widely prescribed for disorders ranging from mild to severe. Well-known examples of psychotropic drugs are Valium®, Lithium, and Prozac®.

2. *Electroconvulsive (shock) treatment* has been used as a last resort in the most stubborn cases.

3. *Surgery* (i.e., lobotomy, in which the prefrontal lobes of the brain are severed) has been in use since the late 1940s to control the most severe forms of emotional/behavioral disturbance. However, it has declined dramatically since the introduction of psychotropic drugs.

#5 — Somatic Therapy

Discipline 1: Drug Therapy

Depression

- There is a distinction between depression caused by medical disorders and/or drugs (see next two items) and clinical depression.

- A variety of medical disorders can result in biochemical changes that affect central neurotransmitters, triggering serious depressive reactions (e.g., AIDS, anemia, asthma, chronic fatigue syndrome, diabetes, flu, rheumatoid arthritis, and syphilis).

- **Drugs that can cause depressive side effects** include antihypertensives for high blood pressure, corticosteroids and other hormones, antianxiety drugs, birth control pills, and alcohol.

- Antidepressant medication is indicated for sustained (not occasional) physiological symptoms that are considered to reflect biochemical dysfunction such as sleep or appetite disturbance, fatigue, decreased sex drive, restlessness or agitation or psychomotor retardation, diurnal variations in mood, impaired concentration and forgetfulness, pronounced loss of ability to experience pleasure.

- Researchers hypothesize that many primary symptoms of clinical depression are caused by abnormal regulation of various neurotransmitters, such as serotonin. Antidepressant drugs are designed to restore normal neural functioning in the brain.

- Antidepressant medications fall into the following two major groups:
  1. Heterocyclics (e.g., Prozac®, Zoloft®, Paxil®); and,
  2. MAO inhibitors (e.g., Nardil®, Marplan®).

- Antidepressant treatment usually consists of starting with low doses of a heterocyclic and gradually increasing the dosage to find an effective level, switching to another heterocyclic, and/or combining with lithium or an MAO inhibitor, if necessary.

#5 — SOMATIC THERAPY

DISCIPLINE 1: DRUG THERAPY

BIPOLAR ILLNESS (MANIC-DEPRESSIVE DISORDER)

- **Some heterocyclics have broad spectrum effects and are called "shotguns", while others are more selective and are called "bullets."**

- Common disorders that may cause mania include brain tumors, central nervous system syphilis, encephalitis, flu, and multiple sclerosis.

- **Drugs** that may cause mania include amphetamines, bromides, cocaine, and steroids.

- Symptoms of mania include a pronounced and persistent mood of euphoria or irritability, and at least three of the following conditions: grandiosity or elevated self-esteem, decreased need for sleep, rapid speech, racing thoughts, distractibility, increased activity or psychomotor agitation, and behavior that reflects expansiveness and poor judgment (e.g., buying sprees).

- **Bipolar disorders are invariably recurring, and thus require ongoing drug treatment.**

- The main drug used to treat bipolar disorder is lithium, which stabilizes mood and prevents relapse.

- If the patient exhibits manic behavior, treatment is begun with both lithium and an antipsychotic drug, which will be phased out once behavioral control has been reestablished. Dosage of lithium is increased gradually to determine the most effective level while avoiding toxicity.

- If the patient exhibits depressive behavior, treatment is often begun with an antidepressant in combination with lithium. A risk of giving antidepressants to a bipolar patient is that it may trigger a shift into mania.

- Some major **side effects of lithium** include sedation, nausea, diarrhea, vomiting, fine hand tremor, and weight gain. Used chronically, side effects include leukocytosis, goiter, acne, psoriasis, diabetes, and kidney damage. **A number of symptoms indicate toxicity, such as lethargy, slurred speech, severe nausea/vomiting, tremor, seizures, shock, delirium, coma, and *death*.**

#5 — Somatic Therapy

Discipline 1: Drug Therapy

Psychotic Disorders

- Psychosis is not an illness, but rather a symptom associated with several disorders. The main indicator of psychosis is **an impaired ability to perceive reality,** which can take such forms as hallucinations, delusions, severe confusion, and an impaired ability to judge or reason.

- The three major psychotic disorders include schizophrenia, mania and/or depression, and psychosis associated with neurological conditions (e.g., head injury).

- **Schizophrenia is considered a recurring illness.** It can be either positive symptom schizophrenia (delusions and impaired thinking; hallucinations, confusion, and impaired judgment; severe anxiety, agitation, and lack of emotional control) or negative symptom schizophrenia (flat emotional state; few or no thoughts or mental activity; emptiness and lack of ability to feel pleasure; psychomotor retardation/inactivity; blunting of perception).

- Antipsychotic medications are either low potency, such as Thorazine®, or high potency, such as Loxitane®.

- Antipsychotic medications have three main side effects: 1) sedation; 2) extrapyramidal (EPS); and, 3) anticholinergic (ACH). These side effects are similar to antidepressants.

- EPS side effects include Parkinson's-like symptoms (e.g., muscular rigidity, tremors, mask-like facial expression, slowed motor responses); uncontrolled sense of inner restlessness; muscle spasms and prolonged muscular contractions; and tardive dyskinesia (a late-onset, often irreversible effect of antipsychotic medication that causes involuntary sucking and smacking movements of the mouth and lips).

#5 — SOMATIC THERAPY

DISCIPLINE 1: DRUG THERAPY

ANXIETY DISORDERS

- The six types of anxiety disorder include 1) generalized anxiety disorder—long-term, low-level, continuous anxiety; 2) stress-related anxiety—e.g., divorce, death; 3) panic disorder—full-blown panic attacks; 4) social phobias—e.g., asking someone out on a date; **5) medical illnesses and medications** causing biochemical changes that produce anxiety symptoms; and 6) anxiety as part of a primary mental disorder—e.g., depression, schizophrenia, substance abuse.

- **Drugs that may cause anxiety** include amphetamines, asthma medications, caffeine, central nervous system depressants, cocaine, nasal decongestant sprays, and steroids.

- **Common disorders associated with anxiety** include adrenal tumors, **alcoholism**, hypoglycemia, hyperthyroidism, and premenstrual syndrome.

- Different anxiety disorders are treated with different classes of drugs. **Even social phobias, the most mild of the anxiety disorders, are sometimes treated with MAO inhibitors (antidepressants) or with beta blockers that slow down heartbeat.** More severe anxiety disorders are treated with sedative-hypnotic drugs like buspirone and/or drugs that address the primary disorder.

#5 — SOMATIC THERAPY

DISCIPLINE 1: DRUG THERAPY

ATTENTION DEFICIT DISORDER (ADD)

- The accepted view is that ADD is caused by a neurochemical disturbance (impaired ability to regulate dopamine and/or norepinephrine in the brain).

- Between 3-5% of children are affected by ADD; as many as 70% of ADD children continue to exhibit symptoms into adult life.

- Symptoms include impulsivity (acting before thinking, poor judgment); distractibility and impaired attention/concentration span; difficulty in organizing tasks and activities; restlessness and "hyperactivity"; impaired emotional control; learning disabilities; and low self-esteem.

- **Both stimulants (e.g., Ritalin®, Dexedrine®) and antidepressants (e.g., Prozac®, Norpramin®) are used to treat ADD children and adults.**

#5 — Somatic Therapy

Discipline 2: Electroconvulsive (Shock) Treatment

- Electroshock as a form of treating manic-depressive patients and those with severe depression was introduced around 1938 by two Italian psychiatrists, Lucio Bini and Ugo Cerletti.

- **Shock treatment is considered the final option**—effective, but costly—for cases that have failed to respond to drug treatment. These cases can include patients with severe or psychotic depression, bipolar disorder (especially catatonia and severe mania), persistent psychosis, and schizophrenia.

- **Shock therapy is considered the primary treatment for patients suffering severe depression associated with other conditions** such as advanced cardiovascular (heart) or cerebrovascular (stroke) disease, because it can lessen symptoms such as hypertension and rapid, irregular heartbeat.

#5 — SOMATIC THERAPY

DISCIPLINE 2: SURGERY (FRONTAL LOBOTOMY)

- Under the influence of neurologists Egas Moniz and Walter Freeman, lobotomies were introduced in the late 1940s and early 1950s as a form of treatment for uncontrollable psychotic and obsessive-compulsive patients. Prefrontal lobotomies involve destroying white matter in the frontal lobes of the brain.

- Some patients showed improvement after the operation, but **others underwent severe and irreversible deterioration of the personality.**

- Lobotomy procedures have declined since the introduction of psychotropic drugs.

INFORMATION SOURCES

LITERARY

Boorstin, Daniel J. *The Creators: A History of Heroes of the Imagination.* New York: Random House, Inc., 1992.

Chaplin, J.P., Ph.D. *Dictionary of Psychology.* New York: Bantam Doubleday Dell Publishing Group, Inc., 1985.

Hirsch, E.D., Joseph F. Kett, and James Trefil. *The Dictionary of Cultural Literacy: What Every American Needs to Know* (2nd edition). Boston: Houghton Mifflin Company, 1993.

Kaplan, Harold I., M.D., and Benjamin J. Saddock, M.D., eds. *Comprehensive Textbook of Psychiatry/VI*, vols. 1 and 2. Baltimore: Williams & Wilkins, 1995.

McGreal, Ian P. *Great Thinkers of the Western World.* New York: HarperCollins Publishers, 1992.

Morse, Steven, and Robert Watson, Jr. *Psychotherapies, A Comparative Casebook.* New York: Holt, Reinhart, and Winston, 1977.

Pocket Handbook of Clinical Psychiatry, 2nd edition. Baltimore: Williams & Wilkins, 1996.

Preston, John, Psy.D., and James Johnson, M.D. *Clinical Psychopharmacology Made Ridiculously Simple.* Miami: MedMaster, Inc., 1990.

Schatzberg, Alan F., M.D., and Charles B. Nemeroff, M.D., Ph.D. *Textbook of Psychopharmacology.* Washington, DC: American Psychiatric Press, 1995.

Trager, James. *The People's Chronology: A Year-by-Year Record of Human Events from Prehistory to the Present.* New York: Henry Holt and Company, 1992.

Van Doren, Charles. *A History of Knowledge: The Pivotal Events, People, and Achievements of World History.* New York: Ballantine Books, 1991.

INTERNET AND SOFTWARE

Compuserve: *Grolier's Multimedia Encyclopedia.*

"Dr. Albert Ellis." http://www.iret.org/ellis.html.

"Gestalt Therapy by Alan Brandis." http://home.navisoft.com/aapa/gestalt.html.

"Gestalt Therapy: An Introduction." http://www.gestalt.org/yontef.html.

"Rational-Emotive Behavior Therapy." http://www.iret.org/faq.html.

notes...

Human Needs Psychology

Human needs psychology provides an answer to the age-old question, "Why do human beings do the things they do?" How is it that one human being will sacrifice his own life for another, while another person will murder a stranger for sheer pleasure? What creates a Charles Manson or a Nelson Mandela? A Jeffrey Dahmer or a John F. Kennedy? A Unabomber or a Martin Luther King? What is the force that drives and shapes all of our emotions, actions, qualities of life, and ultimately, our destinies?

While most of us acknowledge that each human being is a unique and special soul, we also share nervous systems that function in the same way. Every human being, whether a migrant worker or royalty, has the same fundamental makeup. **There are six fundamental needs that every person has in common, and all behavior—** be it from those whom we admire or despise—**is simply an attempt to meet those six needs**. This drive to fulfill our six human needs is encoded in our nervous system.

The means or vehicles by which people meet these six human needs are unlimited. For example, one of the six human needs is the desire for *certainty* that we can have comfort (avoid pain and gain pleasure). Some people pursue this need by continuously striving to control all aspects of their lives—their environment, the individuals around them, etc. While other people may obtain certainty by giving up control and adopting a philosophy of faith. Another of the six human needs is the desire for *significance*—a belief that one's life has meaning and importance. Some individuals will pursue this need by competing with others, or by destroying and tearing down those around them. Others may strive to fulfill this need by way of *connection* to other human beings, or by contributing to others in a meaningful way.

We believe that the force of life is the drive for fulfillment, and that all human beings share this need to experience a life of meaning. Ultimately, however, fulfillment can only be achieved through a pattern of living in which we focus our lives on two primary needs: 1) the need to continuously *grow*; and, 2) the need to *contribute* beyond ourselves in a meaningful way. Unhappiness, emotional distress, and all dysfunctional behavior arise from an individual's inability to find a consistent way to meet his or her six human needs. When our attempts to reach fulfillment fail, we will settle for comfort—or for meeting our needs on a small scale. Every person finds a way to meet his or her needs; the only question is whether they will act in a way that is destructive or empowering to themselves and others.

The goal of six human needs psychology is to help people create additional consistent choices—new patterns that allow them to be fulfilled long-term. Ideally, they will achieve these patterns in a way that feels good; that is good for them; that is good for others; and that ultimately serves the greater good.

Human Needs Psychology

4 Primary Points that Create Change

1 **Determine What Every Person Wants/Needs.**
Every person wants to satisfy their six human needs.

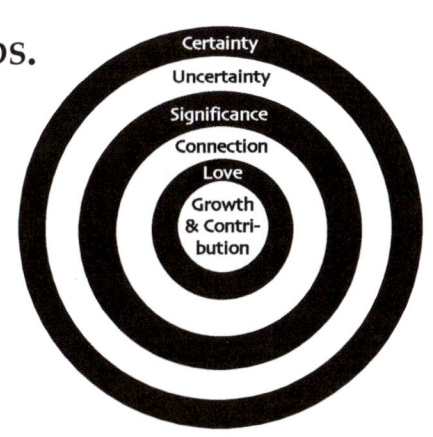

2 **Determine What Prevents People from Being Satisfied.**
The meaning we attach to experiences through the use of three patterns of the triad—*physiology, focus, and language/meaning*—keep us from achieving satisfaction in our lives.

The Triad: The Source of All Emotion is a Constellation of Three Forces		
FORCE #1	FORCE #2	FORCE #3
Patterns of Physiology	Patterns of Focus	Patterns of Language/Meaning

3 **Create Lasting Change Quickly and Powerfully.**
All change is nothing but finding a new pattern of thinking, feeling, and behaving that meets a person's needs on a deeper level than the previous pattern. Then, the new pattern must be conditioned so that it becomes the person's natural and consistent experience of life.

The Seven Master Steps
1. Diagnosis
2. Leverage
3. Annihilate the Pattern
4. Create New and Empowering Alternatives
5. Condition it
6. Test it
7. Create the environment

4 **Maintain an Extraordinary Quality of Life by Creating a Compelling Future and an Identity that Leads to Continuous, Meaningful Growth and Contribution.**
This type of life and identity is achieved by developing a psychology that has four elements:
1) *Hunger and drive* to unleash your passion to maximize your innate gifts;
2) A sense of *absolute certainty* that no matter what life offers you, you will use it—you will find an empowering meaning in any situation and thus, triumph;
3) The ability to experience *tremendous joy* in the process; and,
4) The capacity to *care and connect*—expanding your level of love and compassion for yourself, others, and the gift of life.

Human Needs Psychology

Influencing Motive and Meaning

A life of meaning is created in the moment you decide to serve.

Human Needs Psychology contains the principles, the fundamental understandings, of what drives human behavior: what causes you, your family, your friends, and even strangers, to think, feel, and behave the way they do. Rather than focus on individual tools that may be successful for one person, circumstance, or period of time, Human Needs Psychology focuses on the drives within people that cause them to do the things they do. Most importantly, it operates from the simple belief that **life is determined by the meaning we attach to it;** we are the ultimate arbiters of the experience of our life's meaning. At any moment, we can change the meaning of anything in our lives, simply by changing how we represent things.

Using the understandings of the deepest human needs that are driving us and the process of how we create meaning, it is possible to create global, immediate, and lasting change in anyone regardless of how long they have been engaged in a disempowering pattern.

This school of thought is based on the understanding that while there are many different conscious and unconscious drives among human beings, all human beings have six major human needs that are the underlying driver of every thought, feeling, emotion, and action in their lives. Additionally, Human Needs Psychology recognizes that **all meaning is created by three patterns:** 1) the ways in which we utilize and engage our physiology; 2) the patterns of focus that are utilized in any moment; and 3) the patterns of language/meaning. These patterns create the basis of meaning of and, therefore, how we generate emotions: They are the drivers of the actions and , thus, the results of our lives.

Human Needs Psychology allows for change in an instant. It is possible to break disempowering patterns and behaviors and replace them with ones that will allow an alignment with the drives that make someone feel the way that they do, and then channel them so they naturally move in the direction they desire most—a direction that serves not only them, but all those they have the privilege to touch.

HUMAN NEEDS PSYCHOLOGY

3 DISTINGUISHING CHARACTERISTICS

1 **Nearly all other forms of psychoanalytical orientation approaches use an "archaeological" approach:** They first delve into the roots of initial experiences, usually early childhood. This approach puts the psychotherapist in the position of interpreting what's been created over a lifetime. **Human Needs Psychology focuses on what you are doing right here and now.** *If you're feeling something now, it's because you're doing something now. You change what you're doing now, you'll change what you're feeling. If you change what you're doing with your body you could change what you focus on or how you focus. If you change the language you use, you'll change how you feel.*

2 **Typically, the reference experiences that are being re-worked have to be brought to a conscious level.** This makes consciousness of primary importance. **In Human Needs Psychology, often the effects are made subconsciously.** The therapist can change representations without necessarily requiring a conscious understanding on the part of the subject.

3 **Generally, analytical practices tie the involvement of the therapist as paramount to the success of creating the change. Human Needs Psychology focuses on making the client autonomous** and gives them the tools to be capable of making the change in the event of future difficulties.

HUMAN NEEDS PSYCHOLOGY

3 MANDATES OF HUMAN NEEDS PSYCHOLOGY

1 ALIGN WITH YOUR HIGHER _____: MOTIVE DOES MATTER.

Understanding the driving force in a human being gives you the capacity to find the leverage to change anything.

There is a driving force in all human beings: the driving force for fulfillment. Fulfillment can only be achieved by meeting our spiritual needs of growth and contribution. By meeting these needs intelligently, we not only serve ourselves but we serve society and the greater good.

- Motive determines not only what you'll do, but how you'll go about doing it. There are many motives for anything, but the ultimate motive is always to meet the six human needs.
- To understand the active drive or motive in a person's experience, you must understand their overall Model of the World.
- Our desires drive the story and direction of our lives.
- Motive determines what is driving your behavior: You have to deal with a person's motive so that they don't just trade one behavior for another. Remember, you can change a behavior, but without the motive, the person will just trade one negative emotion for another; one disempowering emotion for another.
- Remember, there is always a higher motive, a global solution: something that will motivate a person more than their pain.

> **WHAT INFLUENCES YOUR MODEL OF THE WORLD**
>
> The originating source of unconditional love; the most desired source of love has had the most influence in shaping your Model of the World. Where people get their love and in what ways they seek it determines a lot about how they live their lives, what they are willing to do to get love, and what they focus on most in life.
>
> For example, if your boss has not spoken to you for three weeks, the feelings will vary hugely depending on what meaning you attach to this. Is he ignoring you, planning to fire you, or is his lack of contact a vote of confidence in your ability? It's a big difference in the meaning and a huge difference in how you feel.

2 MASTER _____. LEARN TO FIND THE EMPOWERING MEANING IN ANY SITUATION AND YOU WILL BE LIFE'S MASTER.

How we feel about our lives has nothing to do with reality, but rather the way we represent reality or the meaning we give to it.

Emotional pain is always the result of constructing and creating a disempowering meaning within ourselves. **Change happens when we value finding a higher level of empowering meaning than the meaning of an illusion of loss.**

Answer(s): motives; meaning

HUMAN NEEDS PSYCHOLOGY

3 MANDATES OF HUMAN NEEDS PSYCHOLOGY (CONT.)

2 **(CONT.)**

In any moment, whether we consider something to be hopeless, challenging, or exciting, instantly changes the experience of our world. We all give meanings at two levels:

1) **FA1 (First Access):** Our bodies are a transformer that take stimuli from the outside world as input and transform it into biochemical and electrical signals that we then, within this physical form, give an initial meaning. This is not something most of us can control consciously. FA1 is the first moment of access where we can begin to change our experience of something. This is the level that we attach language to our experience.

2) **SA2 (Second Access):** The moment we attach language to our experience, the language becomes our experience. It changes our biochemistry and our experience radically.

All change—whether it be the work of Freud, NLP, or Human Needs Psychology—is nothing but the manipulation and transformation of the way we represent things. You can only feel things that you represent. When you change your representation, you change your feelings instantly.

3 **MASTER THE _____ OF INFLUENCE AND CHANGE.**

Utilize tools that will change or influence people's motives and meanings.

To create lasting change, all we have to do is **find a way to fulfill the higher motives** of a human being in a more effective and elegant way (i.e., a Class I experience: something that is good for them, good for others, serves them, and serves the greater good) **and/or change the meaning of the experience** which will change their feelings, emotions, and behaviors, and therefore their results. This can be done very powerfully by changing how we represent anything.

Therefore, any tool that provides the capacity to engage an individual to either unconsciously or consciously change the way they represent any aspect of their lives will change their experience of life. There are unlimited tools in this area.

Answer(s): tools

Human Needs Psychology

The Best of Each of the Schools of Psychology

From the *Psychodynamic School*, we utilize Freud's overall understanding that we have the other-than-conscious mind and that the conflicts between the conscious and unconscious desires need to be resolved. Alignment or congruency is power. This can be achieved in a variety of areas utilizing speaking (especially the form that provides hypnotic input into the individual in order to alter the person's representations and therefore change the meaning and experience of their lives). Six Human Needs Psychology, however, uses this differently from psychodynamics by not having presuppositions that there are only one or two sets of primary drives. We want to customize our work by understanding the conflicts that can occur between conscious and unconscious desires and by utilizing language to radically alter a person's representations.

We honor the *Humanistic School* and the fundamental understandings and tools that can be drawn from it, in that we believe the individual can be the source of healing itself. Our assumption is that people can improve through their own efforts and that we are merely coaches consulting with them on how to maximize the quality and experience of their lives.

We utilize tools from the *Behavioral School* because once we determine the changes that are needed for a person to be more fulfilled, we want to use the tools of conditioning to make them automatic and habitual.

From the *Cognitive School*, we understand and utilize any tool that helps us change the process of how a person represents things or generates meaning. We know that changing many cognitive processes can change the emotions and behaviors that are attached to it.

While we do not believe in drugging someone, from the *Somatic School* we recognize the fact that water, breath, and food are probably some of the most powerful drugs a person consumes. In addition, as an extension of the Somatic School without the downside, we believe that shifting physiology is one of our core focus tools for creating lasting change.

Finally, we honor a new school—*Energy Psychology*—that allows us to utilize precognitive tools, i.e., to change the energy that's trapped in the body that causes the body to represent forms of stress that are then interpreted through patterns of language to produce emotion and behavior.

Some of our favorite tools from each of the schools mentioned above include those of Psycho- and Neuro-linguistics, Neuro-Associative Conditioning, Behavioral Conditioning, and Cognitive and Multi-dimensional or Destiny Technologies.

notes...

HUMAN NEEDS PSYCHOLOGY

ORGANIZING PRINCIPLES

1 **All human behavior is driven by the pursuit to fulfill one or more of the six human needs.** When an event occurs in our lives, we take in stimuli through an internal process. Most people think of this process as *thought* (which includes physiology, focus, language patterns, and belief structures) that creates meaning(s). From this meaning(s) we generate emotion(s); from this emotion(s) we produce behavior(s); and from this behavior(s) we produce result(s).

2 **People are unique and have special abilities to interpret the world beyond their five senses.** Because we can only measure these five senses, we must learn to control them.

3 **People are responsible for their own experiences; no one can make them feel a certain way.** The fact is, we experience what we are *doing*. If a person says "I feel sad," they are actually *doing* sadness. In other words, they are using their body (their breathing, their facial muscles, their voice, their language, and their belief structures) in a way that causes them to feel sad in that moment. Consequently, this feeling can be changed in a moment if a person has a compelling reason to do so (i.e., leverage) and enough alternatives (i.e., new models of the world).

4 **Understanding and consciously utilizing the tools of neurological conditioning** can provide an individual with the capacity to quickly eliminate behaviors that do not support their wellbeing. In addition, this understanding will assist them in creating habits of thinking, feeling, and behaving that support their continued empowerment and capacity to contribute to society in meaningful ways.

5 **Ultimately, individuals always have the power to choose what they think, believe, and feel, regardless of past conditioning.** All change happens in a moment. The moment we change what things *mean* to us, we create a lifelong transformation in our experience.

6 **Meaning leads to emotion and emotion leads to action. All action is** *a cause set in motion* **which will produce a verbal or nonverbal effect.** Continuous actions lead to continuous effects. Continuous effects create a direction in our lives that ultimately leads us to a destination (our personal destiny). By changing the way we process information (i.e., evaluate and create meaning), we change the *source* of our experiences rather than try to change the behavior, which is simply the surface of the problem. Trying to change behavior without addressing the process in which we create the meanings in our lives is merely *cursing the effect while nourishing the cause*.

7 **Creating an empowering meaning is the way to transform someone's experience from pain to pleasure.** We must remember that we can find an empowering meaning in any situation. Pain is the result of a disempowering meaning that we have constructed within ourselves; it is the result of valuing the illusion of loss more than the commitment to find a higher level of and more empowering meaning.

8 **Everyone has the resources within themselves to change,** but these resources may need to be redirected or attached to a new context in order for a person to become empowered and fulfilled.

HUMAN NEEDS PSYCHOLOGY

ORGANIZING PRINCIPLES (CONT.)

9 In their pursuit of fulfillment, most individuals seek to utilize and master a variety of vehicles, such as money, relationships, position, and spirituality. But these vehicles do not provide fulfillment. **The *meanings* we attach to our use of these vehicles gives us greater certainty, significance, variety, connection, growth, and contribution and thus, determines our level of fulfillment.** Quality of life comes down to the quality of the emotions we experience, as well as the vehicles we choose.

Are these vehicles Class I or II (i.e., feels good, is good for you, is good for others, serves the greater good) or Class III or IV (i.e., does not feel good, is not good for you, is not good for others, does not serve the greater good)? The goal is to turn Class III and IV experiences into Class I and II experiences.

10 There are certain emotions that are more valued than others cross-culturally. **These Power Virtues (e.g., faith, compassion, determination, courage) serve as an antidote to disempowering states that cause human beings to fall short of their true potential for growth, contribution, and fulfillment.** Building one's "emotional muscles" and conditioning oneself to live in these Power Virtue states can transform the quality of a person's life. Everything we see, think, feel, evaluate, and experience is filtered through the emotions we experience at a given moment.

11 **Often, people engage in behaviors that violate what they truly value in order to do what is necessary to meet their needs.**

12 **There are a limited number of problems, and there are numerous solutions to each of these problems.**

13 **The strongest force in the human personality is the need to stay consistent with one's identity.** If we shift identity, then we create long-term, lasting change.

14 **Pain by itself is not a long-term reinforcement; only pleasure is.** We must link pleasure to those things that will serve us most. This model uses pain to ignite the change, and pleasure to make it last.

QUESTION: What creates the difference in people?

1. **We all have the *same needs*** (i.e., the operating system); yet,
2. **We have different *Models of the World*** that determine how we will attempt to meet these needs (i.e., the software); and,
3. **We utilize *different states*** consistently within our Models of the World that determine our execution (i.e., the electric current).

HUMAN NEEDS PSYCHOLOGY

SIX HUMAN NEEDS

Need 1: Love/Connection

 PARADOX

Need 2: Significance

- Bonding
- Sharing
- Feeling a part of
- Oneness
- Intimacy
- At one with

- Sense of being needed
- Feeling of importance
- Sense of meaning
- Uniqueness

Need 3: Certainty

 PARADOX

Need 4: Uncertainty/Variety

- Security/survival
- Ability to produce, eliminate, or avoid stress
- Ability to create, increase, or intensify pleasure
- Surprise
- Difference
- Excitement!
- Diversity
- Challenge

You can meet these needs by destructive, neutral, or constructive means.
Potential vehicles for each need are:

Connection/Love	Significance	Certainty/Comfort	Uncertainty/Variety
Sympathy via sickness/injury	"Tear" others down	Control	Alcohol
Negative behavior (crime, drugs, smoking, gangs)	Violence	Consistency	Drugs
Get others to comply with your requests (acceptance)	Negative identity: disease/disorder	Food	"Sabotage"/pick a fight, etc.
Relationships (family, friends, intimate, sexual)	Material possessions	Learned helplessness	New relationship
Spirituality	Accomplishments (e.g., degrees)	Identity or negative identity	New job
Be in natural surroundings ("in nature")	Style	Completion	New location
Join team/club	Development of new knowledge and skills	Faith/belief in guidance	Stimulating conversation
Self-sacrifice	Growing levels of caring or extraordinary compassion		Take on new challenges
Beauty/art	Scarcity (as a criteria for creating a feeling of uniqueness or importance)		Learn!
Pets			Rechunk your focus/tempo of focus

Primary, Essential, Ultimate Needs!

Need 5: Growth   Need 6: Contribution

- If you help others to be fulfilled, you will be fulfilled.
- Consistently give to others that which you wish to receive.
- You have within yourself the resources to feel completely fulfilled in all six categories, in any situation, regardless of how others respond to you. Simply ask the question, "What would I need to believe/appreciate (perceive) or do (procedure/vehicles/approach) in order to feel more fulfilled in this category now?"

You can meet any or all of these Six Human Needs by changing either your
PERCEPTION (belief or appreciation of) or PROCEDURE (vehicles or approach to).

©Lisa Christiansen Companies GPS To Success 1988   Proverbs 28:27

HUMAN NEEDS PSYCHOLOGY

SIX HUMAN NEEDS SUMMARY: THE 4 NEEDS OF PERSONALITY

Need 1: Connection ← *Paradox* → **Need 2: Significance**

Need 3: Certainty ← *Paradox* → **Need 4: Variety**

THE 2 NEEDS OF THE SPIRIT

Need 5: Growth **Need 6: Contribution**

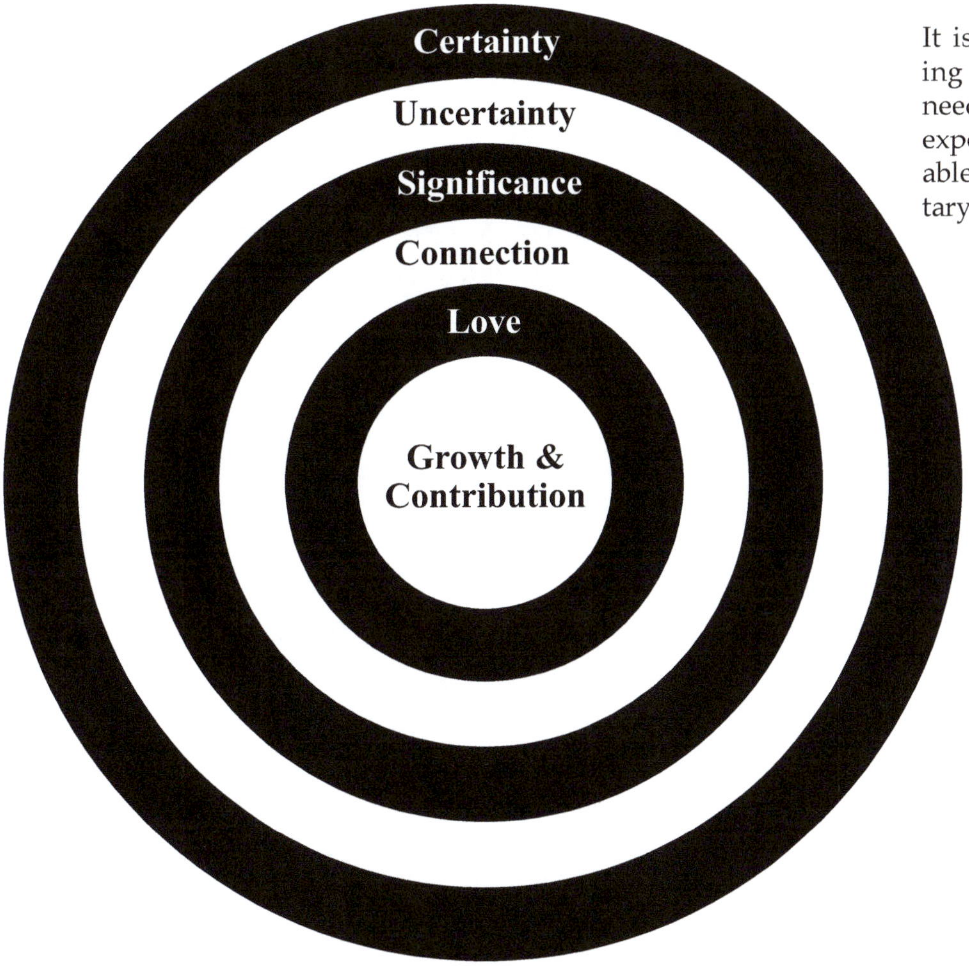

Concentric circles (outer to inner): Certainty, Uncertainty, Significance, Connection, Love, Growth & Contribution

It is only by meeting the spiritual needs that you will experience sustainable joy vs. momentary pleasure.

People find ways to meet these needs in positive, negative, or neutral ways, but every person finds a way to meet them in some way. Any activity, action, or emotion that fulfills at least three needs at a high level becomes, in effect, an addiction. Likewise, people have positive, negative, and neutral addictions. There is always a way to fulfill a need; the skill lies in finding a sustainable way to fulfill it, and in a way that gives you more pleasure than pain.

HUMAN NEEDS PSYCHOLOGY

VEHICLES ANALYSIS CHART

Use this chart to analyze the level of fulfillment that your current vehicles are providing for your life. Through the following process, you can...

1 **Discover *why* you spend your time *where* you spend your time.** Specifically, we constantly move toward those things that provide for us the greatest level of fulfillment. This analysis will show you which of your vehicles provides the greatest level of fulfillment, and what areas of your six human needs are best served by certain vehicles over others.

2 **Clarify what aspect of your six human needs is missing, and then *change or enhance your life* accordingly.**

3 Use this tool as a precise way to take something that you already enjoy and **make it feel *even* better!**

4 Help *expand* the menu of *choices* for your life, and utilize this tool as a testing procedure for the level of fulfillment something will provide in advance of participating in it.

Remember...
By changing your **perceptual** strategies
(i.e., what you notice, appreciate, or believe) or
your **procedures** for utilizing your resources to be fulfilled,
every vehicle can be a level 10.

HUMAN NEEDS PSYCHOLOGY

VEHICLES ANALYSIS CHART

INSTRUCTIONS:

1. Your analysis is state-related, so put yourself in a resourceful peak state before you begin.

2. In the following columns, list your primary vehicles (i.e., vehicles that you use consistently to be fulfilled). Simply look at what you primarily spend your time and focus on (e.g., business/career, earning money, your children, exercise, watching TV, etc.).

3. On a scale of 0-10, place a rating under each of the six human needs determining how fulfilling that vehicle is consistently—not just in this moment, but over time. Give yourself a reasonable range. For example, you might say your career is fulfilling between an 8-9 or 7.5-8.

4. Add the numbers together. (If you gave a range, use the average.) Divide that number by 6 for an overall score that this vehicle provides you.

5. Look at the individual scores under each of the six human needs and write not only the overall score, but which needs this vehicle primarily meets at a high level.

VEHICLE	CERTAINTY	VARIETY	SIGNIFICANCE	CONNECTION	GROWTH	CONTRIBUTION	OVERALL SCORE
READING	7.5-8.5 = 8	7.75-8.5 = 8.125	7.75-8.3 = 8.025	7.5-8 = 7.75	8-9 = 8.5	8.5-9 = 8.75	= 49.15/6 = 8.2 Growth/Contribution
BUSINESS	7.35	7.5-8 = 7.75	7.5-8.5 = 8	8.5-9 = 8.75	8.75	8.25-9.25 = 8.75	= 49.35/6 = 8.2 Connection/Growth/Contribution
FAMILY	7.5-8.5 = 8	7-8 = 7.5	7.75-8.25 = 8	8.5-9 = 8.75	7.5-8 = 7.75	8-9 = 8.5	= 48.5/6 = 8.1 Connection/Contribution
JACUZZI	8.5-9.5 = 9	6.5-7.5 = 7	6.5-7.5 = 7	6.75-7.25 = 7	7.5-8.25 = 8	7.5-8.5 = 8	= 46/6 = 7.7 Connection/Contribution
WATCHING TV	7-8 = 7.5	6.5-7.5 = 7	2.5-3.5 = 3	5.76-6.25 = 6	5.5	5-6 = 5.5	= 34.5/6 = 5.75 Certainty/Variety
EXERCISE	8-9 = 8.5	7.5-8.5 = 8	7-8 = 7.5	7.5-8.5 = 8	8.5-9 = 8.75	7.5-8.5 = 8	= 48.75/6 = 8.1 Certainty/Growth
WRITING	7-7.5 = 7.25	7-7.5 = 7.25	7.25-7.75 = 7.5	6.5-7.5 = 7	7.5-8 = 7.75	7.5-8 = 7.75	= 44.5/6 = 7.4 Growth/Contribution

HUMAN NEEDS PSYCHOLOGY

YOUR VEHICLES ANALYSIS CHART

FOR: _____ DATE: _____

VEHICLE	CERTAINTY	VARIETY	SIGNIFICANCE	CONNECTION	GROWTH	CONTRIBUTION	OVERALL SCORE

VEHICLES ENHANCEMENT PROCESS

HUMAN NEEDS PSYCHOLOGY

You can be completely fulfilled by any vehicle, any outcome, or any activity in your life, if you simply change one of two things: 1) your perception; or, 2) your procedure. Complete the following four steps to immediately enhance your level of fulfillment in this activity, and you will find that it will be effortless to get yourself to do it on a regular basis.

INSTRUCTIONS

1 **CHOOSE A VEHICLE.**
Choose one that gives you a low level of fulfillment that you would like to give you a higher level of fulfillment.

2 **CHANGE YOUR PERCEPTION.**
A. If you change what you Notice, Appreciate, or Believe (NAB), you will instantly change your level of fulfillment. What can you NAB that will absolutely increase your level of fulfillment to a level 8, 9, or 10?

B. Having made this perceptual change, rate on a scale of 0-10 this vehicle's ability to meet each of your six human needs.

C. Describe the most important changes that will allow you to increase your level of fulfillment using this vehicle.

3 **CHANGE YOUR PROCEDURE.**
A. Besides perception, your procedure or your strategy for doing something also affects your level of fulfillment. What new strategies or procedures could you implement that would increase your level of fulfillment? In order for this vehicle or activity to be a level 10, how would you have to change your procedure?

B. Having made this procedural change, rate on a scale of 0-10 this vehicle's ability to meet each of your six human needs.

C. Describe the most important changes that will allow you to increase your level of fulfillment using this vehicle.

4 **DESCRIBE THE MOST IMPORTANT CHANGES.**
A. Having made both a perceptual and a procedural change, rate on a scale of 0-10 this vehicle's ability to meet each of your six human needs.

B. Describe the most important changes that will allow you to increase your level of fulfillment using this vehicle.

Remember...

Every vehicle can be a level 10, at least at times, by changing either your **perceptual strategies** (i.e., what you NAB) or your **procedures** for utilizing your resources in order to be fulfilled.

©Lisa Christiansen Companies GPS To Success 1988   Proverbs 28:27

HUMAN NEEDS PSYCHOLOGY

VEHICLES ENHANCEMENT PROCESS

STEP 1 — Choose a vehicle that currently gives you a low level of fulfillment that you would like to give you a higher level of fulfillment.

STEP 2 — If you change your perception—what you NAB—it will instantly change your level of fulfillment. What can you NAB that will absolutely increase your level of fulfillment to a level 8, 9, or 10?

Vehicle	Certainty	Variety	Significance	Connection	Growth	Contribution	Overall Score

Having made this perceptual change, rate on a scale of 0-10 this vehicle's ability to meet each of your six human needs.

Vehicle	Certainty	Variety	Significance	Connection	Growth	Contribution	Overall Score

Describe the most important changes you can make that will allow you to increase your level of fulfillment using this vehicle.

©Lisa Christiansen Companies GPS To Success 1988   Proverbs 28:27

HUMAN NEEDS PSYCHOLOGY

VEHICLES ENHANCEMENT PROCESS

Besides perception, your procedure or your strategy for doing something also affects your level of fulfillment. What new strategies or procedures could you implement that would increase your level of fulfillment? In order for this vehicle or activity to be a level 10, how would you have to change your procedure?

VEHICLE	CERTAINTY	VARIETY	SIGNIFICANCE	CONNECTION	GROWTH	CONTRIBUTION	OVERALL SCORE

Having made this procedural change, rate on a scale of 0-10 this vehicle's ability to meet each of your six human needs.

VEHICLE	CERTAINTY	VARIETY	SIGNIFICANCE	CONNECTION	GROWTH	CONTRIBUTION	OVERALL SCORE

Describe the most important changes you can make that will allow you to increase your level of fulfillment using this vehicle.

Having made both a perceptual and a procedural change, rate on a scale of 0-10 this vehicle's ability to meet each of your six human needs. Then, describe the most important changes you can make that will allow you to increase your level of fulfillment using this vehicle.

VEHICLE	CERTAINTY	VARIETY	SIGNIFICANCE	CONNECTION	GROWTH	CONTRIBUTION	OVERALL SCORE

HUMAN NEEDS PSYCHOLOGY

THE FOUR CLASSES OF HUMAN EXPERIENCE

Class I	Class II	Class III	Class IV
It feels good.	It does not feel good.	It feels good.	It does not feel good.
It is good for you.	It is good for you.	It is not good for you.	It is not good for you.
It is good for others.	It is good for others.	It is not good for others.	It is not good for others.
It serves the greater good.	It serves the greater good.	It does not serve the greater good.	It does not serve the greater good.
What are the Class I ways you meet your needs?	*What are the Class II ways you meet your needs?*	*What are the Class III ways you meet your needs?*	*What are the Class IV ways you meet your needs?*

Proverbs 28:27

notes...

"There are many ways of going forward,
but only one way of standing still."

FRANKLIN D. ROOSEVELT

Your Model of the World:
The Driving Force of Your Life

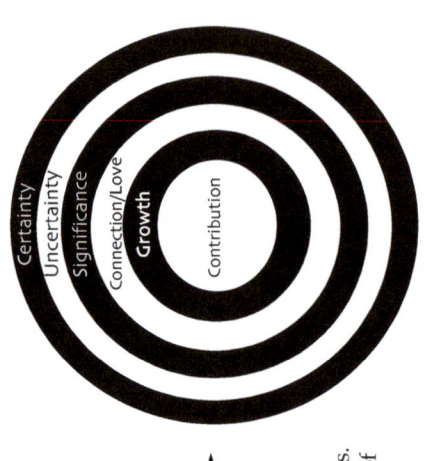

- Certainty
- Uncertainty
- Significance
- Connection/Love
- Growth
- Contribution

HOW →

1. Meet these targets with these beliefs, rules, values, vehicles, primary questions.
2. Avoid these targets with a different set of beliefs, rules, values, vehicles, primary questions.
3. Because these beliefs can be in conflict = Primary Wound.

S.E.E.
Significant Emotional Event
(Reference)

Two Innate Elements
1. DISC
2. Male and Female Energy

Principles that Guide Your Model of the World

1. **Global Beliefs**—factors that will affect your ability to avoid pain and gain pleasure
2. **Values/Rules**—beliefs about what is most important to avoid and/or get in life and when to feel good/bad
3. **Primary Vehicles**—primary ways you have learned to get out of pain and into pleasure
4. **Primary Focus/Questions**—the driving force and the primary pattern of your life
5. **Primary Fear**—the ultimate fear that all people have is loss of love/loss of worth

Lisa's MODEL OF THE WORLD

Lisa has been extraordinarily effective in helping millions of people throughout the world because she has a model of the world that empowers him to make a difference. Many of you have known her for years, what do *you* think is her model of the world?

1 What do you think are her most empowering global beliefs?

_____

_____

2 What do you think are some of her values and rules based on what is most important to do or to avoid doing?

_____

_____

3 What are the primary vehicles she uses to meet her needs?

_____

_____

4 What is her primary focus?

_____

_____

5 What are her primary questions?

_____

_____

6 What are some of the painful references that have driven her? What are some of the pleasurable ones?

_____

_____

exercise

Menu of Ways To Feel Good

Make a list of all the activities that make you feel good.

Activity	Participating in this activity costs money.	I can participate in this activity alone.	I need others to participate in this activity with me.	I can do this activity while doing something else.	I can participate in this activity anyplace.	I can participate in this activity only once in a while.	I participate in this activity anytime.	I participate in this activity frequently.	notes
Remember something that makes me laugh		X		X	X		X	X	
Go water skiing	X		X			X			

exercise
Menu of Ways To Love Yourself

Make a list of all the ways you can love yourself.

To love oneself is the beginning of a lifelong romance —Oscar Wilde

Activity	Participating in this activity costs money.	I can participate in this activity alone.	I need others to participate in this activity with me.	I can do this activity while doing something else.	I can participate in this activity anyplace.	I can participate in this activity only once in a while.	I can participate in this activity anytime.	I participate in this activity frequently.
Look in the mirror and smile at myself		X		X			X	X
Call a close friend	X		X		X		X	X

notes

The History of Psychology: Testing What You Know:

1. Match the name of the corresponding discipline of **Dynamic Psychotherapy** to the name of the respective pioneer/innovator/founder.

    1. Psychoanalysis
    2. Analytic Psychology
    3. Individual Psychology
    4. Holistic Therapy
    5. Interpersonal Psychology
    6. Transactional Analysis

    _____ Alfred Adler
    _____ Eric Berne
    _____ Sigmund Freud
    _____ Karen Horney
    _____ Carl Jung
    _____ Harry Stack Sullivan

CIRCLE THE CORRECT ANSWER

2. The **goal of dynamic psychotherapy** is to help patients become aware of the _____ that cause difficulties.

    A. Behavioral and mental processes
    B. Unconscious Forces
    C. Voluntary and involuntary aspects of human nature

3. Freud's theory of the **Oedipus Complex** refers to:

    A. Repressed love and hostility toward parents
    B. Neurotic symptoms caused by conflicting thoughts
    C. The irrational complications arising out of childhood experience

4. Freud once glibly stated that **"Sometimes a cigar is just a cigar."** This would seem to repudiate his theory that:

    A. Certain changes in a patient are predictable
    B. Many unconscious thoughts, feelings, and impulses are related to sexuality
    C. Dreams often represent wishes

5. One of the major limitations of Freud's **Free Association** therapy is:

    A. Dream symbolism is not universal
    B. It doesn't leave any room for the possibility that all problems stem from deep-seated conflicts
    C. It is not outcome-focused

6. Carl Jung believed that people have **two layers of the unconscious** – they are:

   A. The spirit and the mind
   B. The universal and the personal
   C. The personal and the collective

7. Carl Jung's term for the contents of the collective unconscious (**images or symbols** that represent a specific identity):

   A. Forgotten or repressed thoughts and feelings
   B. Archetypes
   C. General creative life energy

8. According to the discipline of **Individual Psychology**, people are **not guided by unconscious instincts**, but by:

   A. Obsessions
   B. The deepest layers of the unconscious
   C. Conscious values and goals

9. The main **strength of Individual Psychology** is the understanding that people **move away from pain** (specifically the pain of feeling insignificant, i.e an "inferiority complex") and **move toward...**

   A. The anima
   B. Goals that make them feel successful and superior – a.k.a., *pleasure*
   C. Preternatural experience

10. If an **Individual Psychology** therapist were to tell a timid person, **"Don't start doing anything too brave,"** he or she would be using Alfred Adler's technique commonly termed...

    A. Diversion therapy
    B. Reverse psychology
    C. Joining

11. **Holistic Therapy** reinterpreted Freud's psychoanalysis to stress _____ over sexual and aggressive drives.

    A. Security
    B. The deepest layers of the unconscious
    C. Obsession

12. A major **strength of Holistic Therapy** is the understanding of the fundamental, driving **human need** for...

    A. Idealized imagination
    B. Certainty
    C. Cooperation and reciprocity

13. Therapists who favor the **Interpersonal Psychology discipline of dynamic psychotherapy consider diagnostic labeling** to be...

    A. Helpful, necessary, and a positive tool for emotional progress
    B. Unhelpful, restrictive, and dehumanizing
    C. A great way to stabilize behavior in an unuseful way

14. **Transactional Analysis** is based upon the belief that people have **three "parts" or ego states** within themselves:

    A. A child, a parent, and an adult
    B. An ego, a denial and a libido
    C. A conscious, subconscious and superconscious

15. A major **limitation of Transaction Analysis** is that it allows you to **rationalize and justify your problems** by...

    A. Allowing a detailed inquiry of unspecified duration
    B. Blaming your "inner child"
    C. Creating the concept of resistance

16. Match the name of the corresponding discipline of **Humanistic Therapy** to the name of the respective pioneer/innovator/founder.

    1. Client Centered/Nondirective Psychotherapy
    2. Existential Therapy
    3. Gestalt Therapy

    _____ Ludwig Binswanger
    _____ Victor Frankl
    _____ Kert Lewin
    _____ Abraham Maslow
    _____ Rollo May
    _____ Frederick "Fritz" Perls
    _____ Carl Rogers

17. The **Humanist Creed** is based upon a fundamental...

    A. Need for meaning
    B. Respect for patients
    C. Capacity for change

18. A major **strength of Client Centered/Nondirective Psychotherapy** is that it puts the **responsibility where it belongs** – on...

    A. The patients
    B. The parents
    C. Past experience

19. A major **limitation of Client Centered/Nondirective Psychotherapy** is:

    A. Patients often blame their inner child
    B. Patients are encouraged to accept their inner conflicts
    C. Patients receive no advice, interpretation, or direction from the therapist

20. **Abraham Maslow** classified man's basic needs (**Hierarchy of Needs**) into the categories of...

    A. Gluttony and punishment
    B. Abundancy and deficiency
    C. Needs and desires

21. A strength of **Existential Therapy** is that it is **non-judgemental**; therapists do not attach any preconceived meaning to...

    A. Recurring dreams
    B. The meaning of past incidents
    C. Whether or not the existence of others can be proved

22. An **Existential Therapists** can be likened to...

    A. A very kind and supportive friend – whom you are paying to talk to
    B. A guide pointing out a different frame of reference
    C. A coach

23. An organizing principle of **Gestalt Therapy** is that neuroses often comes from **repression** and can therefore be healed by...

    A. Releasing frustration
    B. Exaggerating a neurotic position
    C. Reliving a painful experience

24. While Gestalt Therapists are committed to **open-ended and supportive dialogue** with a patient, they stress the importance of this process over...

    A. Clear direction
    B. A therapeutic outcome
    C. Catharsis

25. Gestalt Therapists will often use **role-playing** as a means to...

    A. Create new internal representations and collapse anchors
    B. Involve cross representational lead systems
    C. Release repressed feelings

26. **John B. Watson, Joseph Wolpe**, and **Burrhus F. Skinner** are all ...

    A. Existential logotherapists
    B. Pioneers of Behavioral Therapy
    C. Developmental psychologists

27. **Behavioral Therapy** is primarily concerned with the various premises relating to the **theory of**...

    A. The pleasure principle
    B. Conditioning
    C. The will to meaning

28. **Skinner** believed in **operant conditioning** – everything that happens within a person is the result of conditioning by...

    A. Internal representations
    B. Childhood experience
    C. Outside forces

28. A major limitation in the organizing principles of **Behavioral Therapy** is that behavior disorders are **learned behaviors, and therefore not caused by unconscious conflict** – a lack of insight, positive regard, etc. In other words behavioral therapists believe...

    A. The symptom is itself the disorder
    B. Disorders are a result of input to sensory apparatus
    C. Disorders are caused by unconscious conflict

29. The four basic principles of **instrumental conditioning** are:

    A. Stasis, conflict, facing and resolving
    B. Programming, anchoring, representations and internal accessing
    C. Reward, punishment, escape or negative reinforcement, and omission

30. **Observational or social learning theory**, which states that people learn not only by doing, but by observing is what we commonly term...

    A. Mottling
    B. Modeling
    C. Reactive learning

31. The greatest **strength of Behavioral Therapy** is that its **focus is on changing behavior**; therefore it is..

    A. Consistent with universal needs
    B. Oriented to the patient's experience
    C. Outcome and results-oriented, as well as measurable

32. Match the name of the corresponding form of **Cognitive Therapy** to the name of the respective pioneer/ innovator/ founder.

    1. Rational-Emotive Therapy
    2. Psycholinguistics

    _____ Richard Bandler
    _____ Noam Chomsky
    _____ Albert Ellis
    _____ John Grinder

33. While **behaviorism sees us as mechanistic**, and **humanism sees us as emotional beings** striving toward self-actualization, **cognitive therapists see us as**...

    A. Soporific
    B. A *thinking* system
    C. Cognitive beings acting out past experience

34. A **strength of Rational-Emotive Therapy** is its methodology for helping to change a person's limiting or irrational...

    A. Obsessions
    B. Fears
    C. Beliefs

35. Match the appropriate **Psycholinguistic term** with its **definition.**

    1. **Syntax** _____ The study of **the sounds of a language**; how words come together to affect their meanings

    2. **Semantics** _____ **The sequence of words** and how the order affects their meanings.

    3. **Phonetics** _____ **The role of meaning** and the analysis of *morphemes* (the smallest units of speech that have meaning.

36. **Cognitive** therapists believe that **changing our thinking process** can...

    A. Dramatically alter our beliefs
    B. Change the way we feel, and thus change our lives
    C. Implicate structural analysis in the process of change

37. The greatest **strength of Cognitive Therapy** is the fundamental belief that **change is**...

    A. The only constant in experience
    B. A material part of stasis
    C. Completely within a person's control

38. The **problem with Cognitive Therapy** is that it fails to recognize that a person's **overall outcome in life is to meet**...

    A. The balance between distress and boredom
    B. Their need for structural analysis and social control
    C. Their Six Human Needs

39. Check the following forms of **treatment** that are considered to be appropriate for **Somatic Therapy**.

    _____ Prozac
    _____ Hot oil massage
    _____ Lobotomy
    _____ Manicure & pedicure
    _____ Electroconvulsive (shock) treatment
    _____ Chinese water torture
    _____ Lithium
    _____ Unleash the Power Within Weekend
    _____ Ritalin
    _____ A week at Namale
    _____ Full body immersion in a bathtub of jello
    _____ A Barry Manilow concert

The History of Psychology: Testing What You Know
Answer Key

1.
1.	Psychoanalysis	_3_	Alfred Adler
2.	Analytic Psychology	_6_	Eric Berne
3.	Individual Psychology	_1_	Sigmund Freud
4.	Holistic Therapy	_4_	Karen Horney
5.	Interpersonal Psychology	_2_	Carl Jung
6.	Transactional Analysis	_5_	Harry Stack Sullivan

2. B
3. A
4. B
5. C
6. C
7. B
8. C
9. B
10. B
11. A
12. B
13. B
14. A
15. B
16. 2, 2, 3, 2, 2, 3, 1
17. B
18. A
19. C
20. B
21. B
22. A
23. C
24. B
25. A
26. B
27. B
28. C
28. A
29. C
30. B
31. C
32. 2, 2, 1, 2
33. B
34. C
35. 3, 1, 2
36. B
37. C
38. C
39. Prozac, Lobotomy, Electroconvulsive treatment, Lithium, Ritalin

Session 1: Decisions & Destiny

Understanding and Directing the Forces that Shape Your Life

To take our lives to the next level, we need to understand that the external world is not the driving force in who we become or what we choose to create for our lives. We all want to take control of the internal forces that shape the direction of our lives so that we may fully realize our emotional, physical, financial and spiritual potential. In this session we will learn the insights, tools, strategies and triggers that can change the quality of your life in a moment.

During the times in life where we get frustrated or overwhelmed or maybe even feel stuck, often there is something that snaps—a moment when everything changes. Regardless of what stage of life you may be in (if you are on a roll and want to continue to the next level, or if you are experiencing challenges you need to turn around), this session of the Ultimate Edge helps you to cultivate the inner strength necessary to forge a path toward true meaning and happiness.

Whether it's changing your body, turning around your finances or finding passion in your relationship, you will discover inspiration for you to accomplish what you've always wanted and shape your own destiny.

> "The possibilities are numerous once we decide to act and not react."
> —George Bernard Shaw

Session 1: Decisions & Destiny
The 3 Pillars of Progress

The road to transformation begins with the foundation of the 3 Pillars of Progress.

First Pillar: Get Focused and Clear, and Make It Compelling

The first step is to clarify the results you desire in your life. What do you want most in the areas of life that are important to you? What is your definition of an extraordinary quality of life? What do you need to take your life to the next level?

Without a clear and compelling vision for what you want today, you won't be able to even find the target of lasting happiness, let alone hit it. Your chances of knowing what your bullseye looks like, however, depends on how honest you can be with yourself. When you've got a clear and compelling vision of what it is you want, it shifts your mind and emotions, giving you the impetus to shift your actions toward your goals.

Second Pillar: Get the Best Tools for Results

Once you've defined your target, you need an effective and efficient game plan to hit it. In order to close the "gap" between where you are and where you want to be, you need a proven map, an effective mentor and training to drive you to take action. Armed with proven tools, high-quality skills, an effective coach to constantly measure your progress and an empowering community to hold you to a higher standard, there is no way that you won't get the results that you deserve!

Third Pillar: Get Integrated and Get Aligned

However, sometimes tools are not enough: you need to unlock what's blocking you and unleash your authentic power. Why is it that sometimes we know what to do, we have great motives for change, and yet we fail to follow through? Or we make changes in the moment, but they do not last long term? What's missing is a practical understanding of human psychology: why we do what we do and how to change it. By understanding your personal blueprint—how you create meaning and emotion and what causes you to think, feel and behave the way you do—you can not only gain the answers to these questions but learn how to create lasting change and fulfillment. Through the process of discovering, understanding and aligning your internal drives, you are able to channel them so that you naturally move in the direction you desire more—a direction that serves not only you but also all those you care about.

Session 1: Decisions & Destiny

Resources vs. Resourcefulness

The biggest illusion we have in life of why we can't achieve something is that we start to believe that we're lacking adequate resources. I don't have enough money. I don't have enough time. I don't know the right people. I don't have the right training. While any of these may in fact be true, there has certainly been something in your life where one or more of the above factors didn't stop you. You found a way. You may not have had the money, but you were creative enough to get it. You may not have had the education, but you found another way to learn a skill.

If the obstacle seems absolutely impenetrable but you're focused enough, will you find a way anyway? Of course you will, if you have enough determination, enough flexibility and enough creativity. The truth is resources are never the real problem. The real problem is a lack of resourcefulness, and the ultimate resource is human emotion. Human emotion is how we get the resources we need. We tend to forget this because we live and operate in a cognitively driven world, that is, we lean on our ability to figure things out. And if we reach a point where it seems like we can't figure out a solution, that's when the illusion of failure keeps us from reaching our goals. But in reality, if we feel strongly enough about something, no amount of time or perceived lack of resources would keep us from achieving what we want.

The mind needs fuel. It operates very differently when you're passionate about something than when you're frustrated, angry, bored or dejected. Your mind will wire itself differently when you're feeling excited, eager, enthusiastic, inspired or engaged in what you want to achieve, like there's a real purpose behind your goals. That passion expands into your thoughts, actions and the way you interact with people.

Change the fuel that drives the mind, and you change the experience of anything you're trying to accomplish. We're either unresourceful or resourceful based on the habit of emotions that we use most often. Once you realize that you are in control of the fuel that directs your thoughts and actions, the next step is to recognize the power of the decisions you make from moment to moment and throughout your life.

Session 1: Decisions & Destiny
Two Master Lessons of Life

Gaining the ultimate edge in life requires mastering two skills: the Science of Achievement and the Art of Fulfillment.

1. **The Science of Achievement**—going from where you are to where you want to be—requires a plan, a specific strategy. You can achieve anything you desire simply by following certain laws. Whether you want to improve your financial outlook, enhance your relationships or sculpt your body into fantastic shape, following a set of scientific principles will guarantee results.

2. **The Art of Fulfillment** means experiencing tremendous joy in the process—so you feel not only the excitement of the pursuit but the enthusiasm and gratitude for the little things in life along the way.

If you're going to feel happy, alive, excited and passionate about life, you must understand that these lessons go hand in hand. Consider the very famous—although they achieve the heights of success, some never feel fulfilled despite the money, accolades and more. Remember, success without fulfillment is the ultimate failure.

Session 1: Decisions & Destiny
The Power of Decision

Can you think about the areas in your life where you feel most fulfilled, be it your relationship, your career, your body or your family? The path to fulfillment is progressive—an ongoing journey or a project that engages your love, passion and time. More often than not, however, you can pinpoint a moment of significant change that inspired or triggered the actions that led to personal achievement. It is in these moments that you align and focus the power of your inner world to accomplish success and fulfillment in the external world.

The goal is to provide you with the knowledge and tools to create and take advantage of these moments of personal empowerment. Utilizing this power—this emotional fitness—to work against fear and doubt and overcome any obstacle allows you to become the architect of your own destiny instead of simply reacting to the forces in your environment.

> **The Ultimate Edge = Psychological Strength**
> Mental edge and focus that maximize who you are, what you're capable of and what you get to enjoy out of this life.

The Power of Decisions

We are able to exercise this emotional fitness and psychological strength through action. Nothing changes without new action. It is also essential to remember that every action is parented by a decision. Before you take action, you have to make a decision. No matter how inconsequential a decision may appear to be, even the smallest decisive notion could change the outcome of your life. It's in your moments of decision that your destiny is shaped.

> **Decisions = Destiny**

Each day we're making new decisions and creating new actions, all fueled by the power of emotion. It is up to us to nurture the emotions that engender a level of positive activity and growth through consistent and focused decision-making. Some decisions may only have short-term impact, and others affect us far beyond what we could imagine in the moment. Either way, remember: decisions are shaping your life's destiny.

Session 1: Decisions & Destiny

The Three Decisions

There are three decisions you're making every moment of your life, either consciously or unconsciously. Developing the capacity to make the changes you want to make in life depends on your ability to become conscious of the decisions that you're making all of the time.

First Decision: What Are You Going to Focus On?

Every moment of your life you have to decide what you're going to focus on. If you don't consciously choose where to point the lens, your brain just goes into the habit of what it usually focuses on. Most people focus on what they're afraid of, and whatever you focus on, you feel. So if you keep focusing on what you fear, you bring it to life. As you think about it, it becomes alive inside of you. On the other hand, if you focus on the potential in an event or situation, then opportunities begin to present themselves.

Second Decision: What Does This Mean?

The minute you focus on something, your mind has to come up with a meaning for it. From an evolutionary standpoint, the human nervous system has to know: is this going to mean pain or pleasure? Whatever meaning you give to an experience, then that experience becomes that meaning because you make it real in your body and mind. If you don't consciously choose what things mean, your old patterns show up. Come up with an empowering meaning, and you change how you'll feel.

Third Decision: What Am I Going to Do?

Once you focus on something and give it a meaning, it produces an emotion. Those emotions filter what you do and trigger action, or even non-action.

If you're angry, are you going to do something different than if you're feeling grateful? If you're fearful, worried or stressed, are you going to do something different than if you feel determined, curious or playful?

It all comes down to these three decisions. They're shaping your life moment to moment. If you take control of them, everything changes. You don't have to wait to be emotionally fit in order to start down the path that will lead to your ultimate edge. You have to decide to raise the standard of what you expect for yourself now. You have to decide that it's time to go to the next level.

Session 1: Decisions & Destiny

The Two Forces that control our decisions

There are two forces that influence every decision we make:

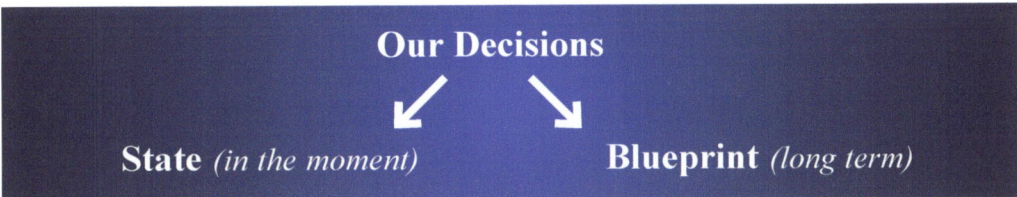

1. State

Ultimately, we want to feel states of empowerment, like confidence, certainty or adeptness, that will positively impact the quality of our decisions most of the time. Few people are in empowered states all of the time. But even "negative" states of emotion—frustration, anger, envy—can sometimes be useful to propel us to make changes. Being conscious of our moment-to-moment state gives us better control over how we feel, hence control over the quality of decisions we end up making.

2. Blueprint

Our Blueprint is our Model of the World—a specific set of beliefs about how we're supposed to be, how life's supposed to be or how other people are supposed to treat us, which determines what we're even willing to consider doing or not doing. In short, our Blueprint will have a massive impact on the decisions we make both in the short term and in the long term because it colors how we look at our lives.

Blueprint: A Brief Introduction

We experience happiness whenever our Life Conditions (what is actually happening with our career, body, relationships, finances, etc.) align with our Blueprint or Model of the World. Since there is no gap between our expectations and reality in this area, we are happy.

$$\text{Life Conditions} = \text{Blueprint} = \text{Happiness}$$

But if there is an area of life that is causing you pain, it's because your Life Conditions do not match your Blueprint.

$$\text{Life Conditions} \neq \text{Blueprint} = \text{Pain}$$

Success Leaves clues
Journal Notes

Session 1: Decisions & Destiny

Your Assignment

Let's Take a Look at Your Life

1. What is an area of your life where you are really happy?

   _____
   _____
   _____
   _____
   _____

2. Why are you happy in this area?

   _____
   _____
   _____
   _____
   _____

3. What is an area of your life where you are not happy?

   _____
   _____
   _____
   _____

4. Why are you unhappy in this area?

   _____
   _____
   _____
   _____
   _____

Session 1: Decisions & Destiny

Three Choices

When we are unhappy and our Life Conditions do not match our Blueprint, we have three choices as to how we're going to handle the challenge:

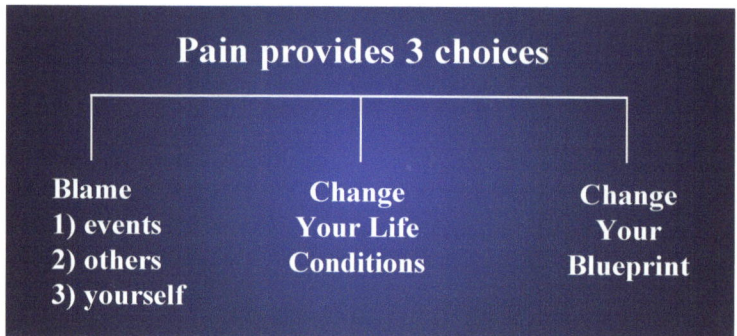

First Choice: Blame

The first choice people have is to assign blame, and there are three things you can blame:

- **Event.** There's a story, something that happened, behind why things are the way they are. However accurate the story may be, blaming an event is convenient because it helps preserve an identity designed to shield us from our true fears: fear of failure and fear of not being loved or accepted.

- **Others.** "I'm in this situation because this person ..." Similarly, the story may be true, but it's convenient and gives you comfort in the moment. "There's nothing wrong with me. It's this other person. There's nothing I need to change."

- **Yourself.** Most people think that this is being responsible, but blaming yourself will not make it better. There's a difference between responsibility and beating yourself up—between "Here's a pattern that I've got to change" and "I'm not good enough."

> **Blame is a choice that doesn't give you anything.**

Second Choice: Change Your Life Conditions

Take a new action, something that will help you make significant progress. If you want to have happiness, you have to understand one thing: progress = happiness. If you feel like you're making progress in an area of your life, you will start to be pleased in that area. You start to get more focused and specific about what you want to change, and you build momentum toward the results you want. If, for example, you want to open your own business, find an achiever to mentor you. Get focused on why you want to make the change and commit to something new in your life.

Third Choice: Change Your Blueprint

Sometimes things are outside of your control, but you CAN control how you configure your rules about how things should be. Your happiness is going to be limited if you want success but aren't willing to ever be judged or want love but distrust the opposite sex. Sometimes adjusting your Blueprint means compromising some of your rules that are difficult for you and others to live up to or are simply impossible to fulfill.

When it comes to the three choices you face on how to handle a problem, the first choice isn't really a choice at all. Blame leaves you stuck, spinning your wheels with no options to change as you tell yourself, "There's nothing I can do about it because …" We all use blame at times, but the quicker you can get out of it, the faster you'll be empowered to either change your life conditions or change your perspective, both of which are real, tangible options that can instantly transform a relationship, your career, your finances or your life.

Success Leaves Clues

Journal Notes

Session 1: Decisions & Destiny
Your Assignment

EXERCISE: Write What an Extraordinary Life Would Be Like for You Today ...

Write a paragraph or two to answer this question: What would your life be like if it was exactly the way you wanted it to be today? In other words, start with the ultimate end in mind.

If your life were extraordinary—life on your terms—what would that look like? How would you change? What would you enhance? Who would you spend more time with? What would you appreciate more? What would you do?

_____
_____
_____
_____
_____
_____
_____
_____
_____
_____
_____
_____
_____
_____
_____
_____
_____
_____
_____
_____
_____
_____
_____
_____
_____

Success Leaves clues

Journal Notes

Session 2: Your Hour of Power

The Key to Personal Transformation & Results

There are two forces controlling every decision in our lives:

> 1. **State:** How you feel in any given moment.
>
> 2. **Blueprint:** Your structure of beliefs and values.

Hour of Power is designed to help you create rituals to condition empowering emotional states. Gaining the ultimate edge in life means experiencing the primary emotions you want regardless of life's events, not just attaining a life that works out every way you want it to. Sometimes, life rains on your parade, but you can control what it means to you. And when you control what it means to you, you have the edge, the ultimate advantage.

To make that happen, you must recapture what's missing—time for yourself, time to heal mentally and emotionally so that consistent space facilitates a shift in your habitual thoughts and feelings. You don't want to wait to attain a goal you've been looking to reach for a long time before you start feeling good about life. You want to direct the course of your life. Fulfillment is not an automatic result of success. Fulfillment is an emotion you must nurture to enhance your quality of life as you work toward your goals and beyond.

Session 2: Your Hour of Power
Take Stock of Your Emotions

Which emotions do you feel on a regular basis? Make a list of all the emotions you consistently experience in an average week.

Empowering/Positive	Disempowering/Painful

Session 2: Your Hour of Power

The Three Patterns that Create Any Emotion: The Triad

Anything in life you want, you only want because of the feeling you think obtaining it will give you. But the truth is that you could have that feeling right now—simply by changing the following three patterns:

1. Your Physiology

- Emotion is created by motion. Whatever you're feeling right now is related to how you're using your body.

2. Your Focus and Beliefs

- Whatever you focus on is what you're going to feel whether it is true or not.

3. Your Language

- Questions: Thinking is nothing more than mentally asking and answering a series of questions. Eliminate any habitual questions that do not serve you (e.g., "What's wrong with me?").

- Words: If you want to change your life, pay attention to the words you repeat to yourself. Certain words can change the way you feel: I think you're mistaken vs. I think you're wrong vs. I think you're lying.

- Incantations: When you repeat a phrase with enough emotional intensity, you start to believe it. Utilize the power of incantations by using the ones that support you the most.

Sample Incantations

"Every day and in every way, I'm getting stronger and stronger."
"At last, at last, the past is past; I've broken free and won. And now it's time to love myself and really have some fun."

Tap Into Your Awareness

Get into the habit of evaluating your triad and conditioning yourself to experience the great emotions you want. What are you doing with your body? What are you focusing on or believing? What are you saying to yourself?

Success Leaves Clues
Journal Notes

Session 2: Your Hour of Power

Your Daily Habit for Extraordinary Health & Happiness

Train yourself to jump out of bed immediately, with no hesitation, and start your day with movement.

Phase 1: Move and Breathe (5 Minutes)
- Keep your shoes beside the bed, and hit the ground running! Get up each day and physically move, going outside and starting with a walk to warm up your body and wake up your metabolism. Take several diaphragmatic breaths in the ratio: inhale for one count, hold for four counts and exhale for two counts.
- Then, for the first five minutes of your walk, practice the pattern of "breathwalking." Inhale four times through your nose, exhale four times through your mouth and repeat continuously.

Phase 2: Get Grateful and Visualize (10 Minutes)
- Think about everything you're grateful for. Start with yourself, and include your family, friends, business associates and special moments in your life
- Visualize everything you want in your life as if you have already achieved it and you are grateful for it. Your brain can't tell the difference between something you vividly imagine and something you actually experience; whatever you focus on, you'll move toward.
- Focus on what you want to create today. What do you want to make happen?
- What do you want to do, achieve or accomplish? See it happening the way you want it.

Phase 3: Use Incantations and Exercise (15–30 Minutes)
- Do your incantations out loud. Speaking engages your physiology and conditions the ideas into your mind.
- Exercise and then celebrate!

Your Assignment

Step 1: Today, keep your eyes open for magic moments.

Step 2: Tomorrow, first thing in the morning, start your day by doing your Hour of Power, 30 Minutes to Thrive or 15 Minutes to Fulfillment.

Your Name

Mission Statement _____
_____
_____

Moving Towards Values & Rules
1
2
3
4
5
6
7
8
9
10
11
12

Moving Away From Values & Rules
1
2
3
4
5
6
7
8
9
10
11
12

My New Primary Question _____

My Power Virtues
1
2
3

My Top Three One Year Goals
1
2
3

My Ultimate Vision
_____
_____
_____

Lisa Christiansen Companies ©

©Lisa Christiansen Companies GPS To Success 1988

Proverbs 28:27

www.ingramcontent.com/pod-product-compliance
Lightning Source LLC
Chambersburg PA
CBHW042036150426
43201CB00003B/39